VICTORY
FROM THE
SHADOWS

First Place, National Federation of Press Women Professional Communications Contest, Adult Non-Fiction Book, Biography, 2020

First Place, New Mexico Press Women Communications Contest, Adult Non-Fiction Book, Biography, 2020

Silver, James McGrath-Morris Award for Published Non-Fiction, A Celebration of Writing by the Albuquerque Museum Foundation, 2019

New Mexico/Arizona Book Award Finalist, Biography, 2019

VICTORY
FROM THE
SHADOWS

GROWING UP IN A NEW MEXICO SCHOOL FOR THE BLIND AND BEYOND

GARY TED MONTAGUE
AND
ELAINE CARSON MONTAGUE

©2019

by Gary Ted Montague and Elaine Carson Montague
Cover Art by Michael Nail
Cover Design by George Paloheimo Jr.
Trade Paper Edition 2020
Kindle Version 2020

Albuquerque, New Mexico
ISBN 978-0-9985725-3-6

DISCLAIMER

These are the authors' recollections presented as creative nonfiction. Some names, locations, and identifying characteristics have been changed to protect the privacy of those depicted. Dialogue is from memory or imagination. To include facts about blindness in New Mexico and the history of the school, some facts are introduced at times appropriate to advance the story. The packet of letters is real. It was discovered more than sixty years after the letters were written by Gary and his teachers. Some language and attitudes reflect those of the times.

Praise for Victory from the Shadows

Victory from the Shadows tells the heartfelt tale of a special boy's journey to adulthood. Gary Ted Montague never let impaired vision stand in the way of his education or prevent him from finding true love. This is a story of strength, resilience, and optimism. The book offers rare insight into life at the New Mexico School for the Blind and adventures that came with growing up in the rural southwest.

Anne Hillerman, *New York Times* best-selling author of the
Leaphorn, Chee and Manuelito series

Victory from the Shadows is a poignant story about personal strength and persistence. It offers inspiration to people who face any kind of disability, and it enlightens everyone to the emotional hurdles that accompany physical challenges. This book will touch your heart.

Loretta Hall
Award-Winning Author of
Space Pioneers: In Their Own Words

This book vividly delivers the experiences of a person with a disability from an isolated ranch to New Mexico's School for the Blind to a rich life beyond. The Montagues' story spans time from before disability awareness, then the emerging societal understanding of disability, to today's wider recognition of the social, educational, medical, and legal implications of disability.

Ruth Luckasson, J.D.
Distinguished Professor
Chair, Department of Special Education
University of New Mexico

I thoroughly enjoyed *Victory from the Shadows* by Gary and Elaine Montague. The story is rich with New Mexico rural history during the mid-20th Century. Even more, it's a compelling story of personal struggle and eventual triumph. The depiction of life on the family's eastern New Mexico ranch and later the stories of life at the New Mexico School for the Blind are finely told and gripping in their emotional intensity. This is an excellent addition to the annals of New Mexico history.

Rob Spiegel,
Award-Winning New Mexico writer

Victory from the Shadows is a heartwarming memoir dealing with blindness and the perseverance of the author in overcoming obstacles and stereotypes. The author shares his unvarnished story and captures a detailed look at New Mexico's history of dealing with visually challenged people. The reader can't help but be drawn into his story.

Larry Greenly
Award-Winning Author of
Eugene Bullard: World's First Black Fighter Pilot

To the casual reader, Gary Montague's trials are the consequence of limited sight, but his story is much more profound than the determination of a man to bear up under physical adversity. Gary's life is rich with powerful lessons, lessons that speak to the power of determination and optimism and the unwavering resolve to live with dignity and self-respect.

Fredric K. Schroeder, Ph.D., President
World Blind Union

Victory from the Shadows captivated me. I started reading and could not stop, finishing it in less than a day. A story of challenge and courage, it shows that a determined person can develop and define himself despite the restrictions society might try to place upon him because of a perceived disability.

Judith Avila, best-selling co-author of
Code Talker: The First and Only Memoir by One of the Original Navajo Code Talkers of WWII

DEDICATION

Blindness lies along a continuum. It is not always the total absence of light. It was the reason I was uprooted from my home and transplanted into an environment both strange and demanding at age eight. My uncle helped me learn to tackle whatever tasks present themselves. I tip my cowboy hat to Uncle Clyde Montague, who believed in this nephew, one who happened to have low vision.

Gary

Clyde Montague

ACKNOWLEDGEMENTS

The authors thank each other for the ups and downs of the thousands of hours required to bounce around ideas, pull out long-forgotten memories, interview family members and Gary's fellow students, study photographs, and research historical records and current best practices. We used imagination while staying as close to the truth as possible.

We thank our cover artist, Michael Nail. Elaine met him at the the 2018 New Mexico Arts and Crafts Fair, where he won first place in the Best Drawings category.

Friends and colleagues encouraged us along this path, too many to mention but too important to forget. John Bruce Cresap gave insights into rural life and the longstanding friendship of our families. Tarrae Bertrand Levine furnished a videotaped interview with Hazel and Tood Montague which provided language samples and tales. Tom Martinez supported peer memories and braille details. A recording of Charlie Maes reviewed history of the New Mexico School for the Blind (NMSB) physical plant, woodworking, and student life. Barbara McDonald's commemorative book, *Weavers of a Tapestry of Time*, provided one hundred years of school history.

Marjorie McCament wore her distinguished educator hat as she reread our initial effort through three revisions. Elaine's former students, Leslie McMurtry and Justin Calles, offered critical suggestions for improvement of our first effort. Kathy Kuenzer and Nancy Roeder encouraged our dream from the book's birth. Questions from Stan Sager, Jimmy Ning, and Patricia Newman helped us be more direct. Loretta Hall taught us focus and said she was inspired. Dr. Ruth Luckasson endorsed the need for our work. Editors Gabriella Savarese, Rob Spiegel, and Larry Greenly were just fussy enough to make us polish. Members of critique groups (UCI, St. John's, and Wordwrights) and SouthWest Writers offered unselfish advice.

We thank Historic Albuquerque, Incorporated, for filming and posting part of Gary's oral history online at https://binged. it/2jzo1yc and the Historical Society of New Mexico for supporting our project with a Nina Otero-Warren Grant.

We greatly appreciate the strong, kind words of the foreword written by Fredric K. Schroeder, Ph.D., President, World Blind Union.

We thank the American Foundation for the Blind and American Printing House for the Blind, the National Federation of the Blind, and the New Mexico School for the Blind and Visually Impaired and its foundation for their long commitment and service.

We thank God that so many people believed in this project and stepped up to help in unexpected ways. Gary cherishes the love of three strong women: his mother, Hazel; his wife, Elaine; and his favorite teacher, Miss Brown.

CONTENTS

Why Shine a Light on This Life Now?

My wife, Elaine, and I talked about friends we had not seen for years. It was early evening. She sat at the computer. I knew she had something besides old friends on her mind and was ready when she asked a familiar question.

"Honey," Elaine asked, "you have a fascinating story. Are you ever going to write it?"

"No, I am not." I was definite.

"Do you mind if I do?"

"You go right ahead."

"Well, then, you just tell me where to begin."

I heard challenge in her voice.

My story was personal, and I planned to keep it that way. Elaine insisted we could encourage others who struggle with vision loss and, at the same time, preserve history. We could voice important issues and lead by example.

Before I started primary school, I realized that, even with glasses, I could not see as well as my twin sister, Jo Ann. As we played, a softball bounced off my chest. It disappeared in the dirt. I could not find it, but Jo Ann ran near me and picked up the ball. The eye doctor explained to Mother that I have low vision, what some call partial sight, because I see more than light but have a visual acuity of about 20/500.

I can see a doctor hold up one or two fingers during an exam, but I cannot perceive objects and colors as clearly as most people. I cannot always read the largest letter on an eye chart. I recognize a friend across a table by outline and voice, and I get ink on my nose when I read newspaper headlines, even with glasses or a hand-held magnifier. In a dimly lit restaurant, I cannot perceive tables, chairs, or customers until I am there for quite a while.

Despite the challenges of low vision, I earned a Bachelor of Arts degree in Secondary Education from the University of New Mexico long before the passage of the Americans with Disabilities Act or widespread use of white canes and guide dogs. I had the help of almost 300 volunteer readers. I have now been married to Elaine for about six decades. I retired from Sandia National Laboratories after a career of thirty-two years as an education tech.

Why shine a light on this life now?

- To celebrate the human spirit
- To encourage those facing a barrier
- To urge perseverance with integrity whatever the challenge
- To embolden advocates for change
- For those who felt abandoned or alone as a child
- For those with children who face abrupt life changes
- For parents, fellow students, and teachers in inclusion classrooms
- To demonstrate that persons with little or no vision can live fulfilling lives
- To thank those who gave so much to me
- To preserve important educational history

- To recognize the value of volunteers
- To hearten parents waiting in the eye doctor's office
- To reassure grandparents fearful about the future of a child with poor sight
- To bolster older folks who are losing vision
- To inspire service providers working with children
- To speak as someone who understands the complexities of being a child who must have educational modifications

iv

FOREWORD

Gary Montague's story is equal parts uplifting and heartbreaking. It is the struggle for social acceptance; the struggle to be taken seriously and to be recognized as an equal; the story of a man— disciplined and sincere—ready to assume life's responsibilities. He struggled at every step along the way. To the casual reader, his trials are the consequence of limited sight, but his story is much more profound than the determination of a man to bear up under physical adversity.

Gary's story is one of a man battling to overcome the pain and disappointment of prejudice and low expectations— the unthinking and unwarranted dismissal of society—the assumption that limited sight means a limited, lesser place in the world. If his story were to end there, it would tell the story of crushing disappointment and grim acceptance; but it does not, and that is what makes his story powerful and profound.

His story is one of human resilience and ingenuity: the ability to find solutions on his own; to find ways to compete and to excel; to build a future; to marry and live a productive life. It is the story of a man, rich with humor, love and compassion, facing a lifetime of adversity, adversity that batters his heart and soul but cannot crush them, cannot take away his spirit and humanity. His life is rich with powerful lessons, lessons that speak to the power of determination and optimism and the unwavering resolve to live with dignity and self-respect.

Fredric K. Schroeder, Ph.D.
President, World Blind Union

PERSEVERE WITH INTEGRITY
WHATEVER THE CHALLENGE

New Mexico, USA

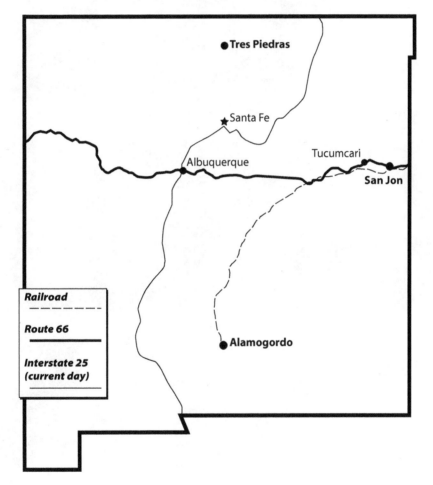

Tres Piedras

Santa Fe

Albuquerque

Tucumcari

San Jon

Alamogordo

Railroad

Route 66

Interstate 25
(current day)

1 THE LIGHT SWITCH

The train screeched to a stop exactly eight hours after I waved goodbye to Dad and Sis at midnight. Through the window, the New Mexico desert looked flat and sandy like home. I pushed at my glasses and squinted to see dark-blue mountains along the horizon.

Mom and I stepped down from the train and headed for a big station wagon with a driver named Gabriel. Wood covered the wagon's sides. I tested it with a finger, then laid my palm on the smooth finish.

"What's this?" I asked Gabriel as he loaded our bags.

"A Ford Woodie. A dandy. Glad we have this old gal because they're hard to get ahold of these days. The war, you know."

It was 1944, the morning after Labor Day, and I was eight years old. Gabriel guided the Woodie out of town and over a cattle guard. I knew that sound and leaned toward the open window to see a wrought iron fence with points. We stopped at a red brick building larger than my old school, and the fragrance of roses made me rub my nose as I got out of the Woodie. Or maybe it was the grass. Our horses and cows would love grazing here, I thought, but we had no flowers at home.

Gabriel laughed. "Welcome to the New Mexico School for the Blind. We call it NMSB. When we forget that, we say Alamo."

I stretched my neck to see all around. My stomach rumbled. I thought about the Alamo.

"Mom, did Davey Crockett die here? I thought that was in Texas."

"It was. This Alamo is a nickname for Alamogordo, New Mexico."

She gave me peanuts to munch. I missed feeding my dogs.

Sturdy shoes tapped concrete, and a hand touched my shoulder. I held still so I would not flinch.

"I'm Mrs. Briggs, your housemother. We're glad you're here, Gary. Come with me for breakfast, then we'll look at your room in the Kindergarten Building."

Kindergarten? Wrong. I was eight. And what was a housemother? I saw buildings but no houses. She was friendly, but my heart somersaulted, so I squeezed Mom's hand on the way to the dining room. We passed quiet lines of boys and girls with grownups. Some touched the shoulder of the person to their right.

Mrs. Briggs leaned toward me. "Our students who can see help the ones who can't. Everyone is on the way to chapel service. That's how we begin each school day."

A school with its own chapel must be special. We sat at a long table. Mom nibbled on toast and talked with the housemother, but I ate a big breakfast. Mrs. Briggs took us to the second floor of the Kindergarten Building, where I saw a bathroom with several stalls. She stopped us in the fifth bedroom. I caught the metal shine of four steel beds, like ones in an army movie.

"This is your bedroom, Gary. I live down the hall. Twenty boys live in this building."

This was not kindergarten because Housemother Briggs said the boys were six to ten years old. Twenty boys were a lot. Did they all come on the train with their mothers?

Mom unpacked my suitcase. Shoes went on the bottom of a locker, shirts and pants on hangers, and the rest on a high shelf that I could barely reach. I didn't bring any toys from home. I wondered why the housemother called it a locker since there was no lock. I breathed fast and wanted to cling to Mom but knew better than to act like a little kid. I pretended to be brave.

Twenty boys. At home, all I had was my twin sister, Jo Ann, and my parents. It was quiet in the building now. What would it be like when the other boys were here?

The school secretary lived on the first floor next to an office and a large playroom. I didn't see any toys. The basement had a smaller bathroom and storage. I thought about what I had seen. My bedroom was in a building with two inside bathrooms and no outhouse. It was called the Kindergarten Building, but it wasn't a kindergarten. I had a locker without a lock and a housemother who did not live in a house.

Mrs. Briggs left us in another large building, where I sat in Mrs. Cole's classroom and bent close to read out loud, solve arithmetic problems, and show her what I could do. Mom listened from the back of the room. Mrs. Cole chuckled and patted my hand. At lunch, I met three boys who were going to be my roommates. They filled me in about classes, meals, and chapel and how important it was to be on time for everything. Bells rang for class changes and sounded like the whistle we all wanted to blow at the end of recess at my old school.

I never got to play that day. I figured they forgot I rode a train for hours. After lunch, I sat alone by a window and was almost asleep when a lady came to ask more questions.

Late in the afternoon, Mom and I walked a mile to a café in town. The temperature was warmer in Alamogordo than at the farm. I was tired and wanted to go home, but she told me I would stay at this school until Christmas—September, October, November, December. Mom said everyone would be glad to see me when I came for Santa Claus. We laughed when I called our Jell-O nervous pudding.

Our hike back to school seemed longer than it had been to the café. When we returned, my roommates were in bed.

Mom said, "You boys will be good friends with Gary. He and I need to say goodnight now. I'll send him a box of cookies he can share with you."

She straightened my top sheet and tucked it and the light wool blanket around me. The sheet was smooth. Her hands were strong. She had not pulled my covers close to my body like that before.

"Goodnight, Gary. I need to leave now."

My insides pounded.

My voice cracked. "Can't you stay longer?"

I was wide awake. Mom looked beautiful as she kissed my forehead. She switched off the light. The darkness frightened me as I heard her footsteps fade away.

My mind swirled with questions. What else would happen?

San Jon High, Junior High, and Elementary Schools, and San Jon
Schools Administration - Elementary in back at left side
of high school. Courtesy of San Jon Schools

NMSB aerial view, courtesy of NMSBVI
and Historic Albuquerque Incorporated (HAI)

2 STAYING POWER

On the piney Tres Piedras homestead in north central New Mexico, Mother sewed clothes for my sister, Jo Ann, and me. Old photos testify our outfits were coordinated since we were twins, but we were too young to appreciate Jo Ann's crocheted collars or my handmade caps. Mom carried water, heated it over an open fire, and scrubbed the family clothes outside on a washboard, then hung them to dry. She pressed shirts, pants, and dresses with a flatiron heated on a wood stove. She killed and plucked chickens and cooked meals that always included dessert. She swept the dirt floor several times a day. She burned trash in a fire outdoors and made lye soap. In the fall of 1936, when I was born, she picked and sold piñons to supplement Dad's income.

Mother's name was Hazel Bernice Moore Montague. She was a high school graduate and had been married almost ten years to my father, a hardscrabble farmer and cowboy. She was not yet thirty. Mother read her Bible by the kerosene lantern at night and prayed silently for her family.

Dad loved our mom. When they met, he thought she was the prettiest gal in the eastern New Mexico town where his family lived. He loved us babies, too, and made jobs for us as soon as we could handle them. A cowboy-farmer like many of his brothers, he fought dry earth and depended upon rain to bring forth feed for livestock and food for his family. And he did it for long hours every day. He bent his back to build rail fences and corrals, lift and repair broken equipment, catch and break horses, and plow fields. His ingenuity and love for vehicles kept a '29 Chevy automobile running. He built our furniture and kept the rain and sand out of our house. People called him Tood, but his name was Grant Thomas Montague. Born in Oklahoma in 1908, the same year as Mother, Dad's mom pulled him out of school in eighth grade because he refused to wear reading glasses to correct a slight vision problem. She told him to get a job. He did.

He farmed the fields, drove tractors and combines for farmers, and built the world around him with his hands. My father was part of rural America and spoke a dialect loosely called "country." An excellent horseman, he loved animals, the soil, and his family, but he had pride and a stubborn streak that sometimes became a hindrance.

I was born in a hospital in Alamosa, Colorado, when the nation had emerged from the Great Depression. Mother was bedridden much of the ninth month of her pregnancy and did not know she would have twins. Dad rented a place in Alamosa, the nearest town, so Mom would be close to a doctor. This is how my sister and I came to be Coloradans instead of New Mexicans. Dad commuted by horseback sixty miles from Alamosa to care for livestock and fields.

My sister, Jo Ann, came first into the world. Seven minutes later, the doctor used forceps to help me. He gave me oxygen because I had trouble breathing and was a bit blue. Smaller than healthy Jo Ann, I did not leave the hospital when she did. Mom said she prayed for me and read the Bible as much as she could. No one knew if I would make it, but I grew stronger. We moved home to Tres Piedras. That is Spanish for Three Rocks and sums up the desolation among the pines.

A few weeks after we returned home, Jo Ann and I were sleeping on a high bed while Mom washed diapers outside. Despite chairs pushed against the bed to catch us, I fell off. Mom found me under the bed with the back of my head against the wall. My color was bad. And there was no doctor for miles.

The ghost of guilt haunted my mother for years as she wondered whether that blow to my head damaged my eyes.

Dad, however, thought illness caused my poor eyesight.

One terrible winter night when I was eight months old, a brutal snowstorm raged. Wet flakes fell fast and heavy. The sky was ebony, and Mom and Dad could not be sure what dangers lay beneath rising drifts. My fever climbed higher, and I cried, coughed, and struggled to breathe. They tried all they knew to help, but I got worse. Dad frantically saddled the mare to ride to our closest neighbor, Dude Newsome, who had a way with doctoring.

The snowfall was dangerously thick. In the blackness, it was impossible for Dad to keep his direction. He had to depend on Ball-ee, his bald-faced mare with a name sounding like an umpire calling "Ball three," to find the way. Just as he trusted she would, Ball-ee went straight through the violence of the storm. Dad ached from the freezing cold, so Dude told him to stay inside. Dude rode to our place and tended me around the clock for three days, putting mustard plasters on my chest and feeding me burnt whiskey.

The first time I heard the story, I was incredulous. "Burnt? Did I get burned? Did I drink the whiskey?" I asked. It turns out that a teaspoon of bourbon warmed over an open burner was Dude's medicine for pneumonia. My parents were certain Dude and Ball-ee saved my life, but they also wondered how much the high fever contributed to my vision problems.

When I was three, Mom and Dad decided to give up the homestead land and move where the weather would be warmer and life less difficult. The four of us moved to eastern New Mexico near the town of San Jon, pronounced h-o-n-e, thirteen miles from the Texas border. The origin of the name is not known. Old-timers think San Jon means big ditch, but there was none. The first postmaster chose the name. The town was founded with the advent of the railroad in the early 1900s. When we arrived in 1939, it was a commercial hub along Route 66.

When I was eight, I moved again. On the day before Labor Day, Mother explained, "You need teachers who are trained to teach kids who can't see print well enough to be good readers. You must read well so you can be on your own when you grow up."

I would attend the New Mexico School for the Blind in Alamogordo, 300 miles to the south. Mother would take me on the train. I paid close attention because she called me "Gary" instead of "Son," and her voice told me she was serious. I was shocked and confused.

It was a sunny Sunday afternoon without much breeze, common to New Mexico, with warm days and crisp, cool, early fall nights that tickle bones with unexpected chilliness. An hour or so after Mom told me the news, I lay in my screened front-porch bedroom and wondered why I did not know anything sooner, why I did not guess something was up. Where was this Alamogordo place, and what was so different about it? I felt excited about the train ride. Questions flooded my mind, questions I dared not ask. Were we going to live somewhere else? Sis came in, and we talked, but what about? Mother said I would go, and that was the way it would be.

Dad did not say a word.

It took decades before I pieced together hints, piecing them one at a time like the squares of Mom's quilts, that Mom and Dad had disagreed strongly about her decision.

3 NIGHT ADVENTURE

Close to midnight, on my eighth Labor Day, September 4, 1944, I huddled with my family in the only seat of our black '38 Chevy pickup. We parked at the train depot in Tucumcari, twenty-some miles west of our farm. The grumbling chi-cha of the coal-burning steam locomotive broke the silence, and I jumped at the suddenness of a whistle blast. Then came the bright light of a gigantic engine, which I knew pulled a long string of cars beyond the glare. We climbed out of the truck. A wave of heat washed over me. I adjusted my glasses and stared at the mass of steel that shushed and clattered in front of me, vibrating the ground under my feet.

I had seen lots of trains and liked to hear them come nearer and nearer with all their power. Sometimes I caught the gleam of an engine flying by on the railroad tracks that ran through the middle of our land in eastern New Mexico. The engine usually just chugged along so I could make out the cars from about a dozen steps away. Sometimes Dad helped us kids put pennies on the tracks so that a train could stretch them. Some disappeared as the heat stuck them to the wheels. I wondered who found them.

Though I spent my days tending chickens or helping milk our thirty-eight dairy cows, I dreamed of being a train engineer taking riders to faraway places to meet a king. Maybe I was helping a famous doctor bring medicine to a sick old grandma who lived by herself and would die if I did not get him there fast. Masked bandits on horseback would attempt to halt my train with pistols, but I never stopped. I listened for the pounding of horses' hooves over the roar of the train because my eyesight would not let me see outlaws who rode through the low-growing grama grass of the Great Plains prairie.

I jumped up and down at the station. My fingers twitched and quivered with the anticipation of a big adventure with my mother—our first train ride. Steam swirled around the door of our coach. The Golden State belched a strong, unpleasant odor that reminded me of hay stacked to cure. Smoke from burning coal smelled like old, damp paper. The odor and the steam made me eager to climb the steps.

I was so excited that I cried out, "Let's go, let's go!"

It had seemed like a normal Labor Day on the farm until Mom and I packed. We fed the animals and cleaned the pens. Mom baked a tall fudge cake with thick icing, and Jo Ann and I licked the frosting bowl clean. We had all my favorites for supper. It was the kind of meal Dad called larrupin' chuck.

Now we were saying goodbyes at the station. Dad held up an open hand and made me laugh when he told me to be extra careful.

He joked in his peculiar brand of country English, "Be keerless, and I'll see ya when I see ya."

Mother did not laugh in her usual way when he murdered the English language. We all kissed and hugged. She and I followed a broad-shouldered redcap as he carried my big suitcase and my mother's little one up the steps and into the car. We sat in the first seat by the door, in front of a group of soldiers. My heart pumped. My stomach clinched and twisted into a knot and would not stay where it belonged. Why weren't Sis and Dad coming? I was confused but thrilled.

The conductor checked our tickets. His dark sleeve with shiny buttons brushed past my cheek and smelled of train smoke. He smiled at me under a hat with a decorated bill. I could not make out the pattern but knew the trim must be real gold.

A man wearing a striped ball cap stepped into our car and reached above the windows to fiddle with something. I learned he was the brakeman who checked the emergency braking system, which worked with a thin cord that had to be just so before we could leave.

The train growled to move. We waved, knowing our people were on the other side of the darkened windows. I felt cold air rush in and heard louder clackety-clacks each time someone entered or left our train car from either end. We ate some of the peanuts Mom carried in her purse.

She said the soldiers on the train looked young and might be going off to war. They did not know when they would see their families again.

Would I see Dad and Sis again? My stomach turned over, and I was afraid I would be sick. The uniforms and hats the travelers wore caught my attention. I was used to cowboys, but not so many military fellows. They seemed full-grown to me. Brown cloth hats pointed sharply to front and back. Dad had told me army guys work for Uncle Sam, and Sam works for us. I looked, but I could not tell if Sam was with them.

Mom patted my knee and told me I would be happier than I was when my sister and my friends skipped a grade ahead of me in school.

"I loved my teacher, Mom, but I didn't want to be stuck with the babies. Is that why I'm on this train—because I failed?"

She assured me I did not fail. "You just couldn't see the books like Jo Ann and the others, so you could not go on."

"But I always got A for oral work." My San Jon teacher wrote "Does his best" or "Tries hard" for written work, and I got F or D in art. How could I draw and paint well? Color inside the lines? Cut out the shapes and glue all those little papers? My hands were fine, but those thin papers rumpled and were too small. I did great with wood and a saw, and I knew how to fit pieces together, but they did not let me do that in school. I wore glasses, but the doctor had me also wear a patch to correct the eye that turned to look toward my nose. I didn't like that patch. Everyone stared at me. I bent over to write in my Big Chief tablet. The last reports showed I was promoted from primary to first grade, but Sis was going to second. I felt miserable.

When I looked at a moving train from our home, I saw one long black ribbon against a light sky. Only when the train stopped could I distinguish separate cars with spaces between them. To be safe and see the moving train, I stood about ten or twelve steps from the tracks, which was about twenty feet. Jo Ann and Dad could see the same thing from about 500 feet, half the distance from the tracks to the big elm south of the house. Dad taught me to measure distances by counting steps. From our back door, I could see the height of the well house with its one-thousand-gallon storage tank on top and knew it took about 100 steps to get there.

As Mom and I talked on the train, I thought of a funny incident involving my shoelaces. My teacher leaned over to help the boy next to me, but I did not see her. I turned sideways and bent down to tie them. As I sat up, my head caught under the teacher's skirt, and I saw her underwear. I got out of there as fast as I could.

"Gary!" she said.

I was scared she'd be mad, and I'd be in big trouble, but she tugged on her skirt and walked away. I was relieved.

I pulled Mom's sleeve and asked, "Am I dumb?"

"No, Son. You are not dumb. You need to be courageous like these soldiers who left their homes to go to war. I told you I had hard times growing up because your granddaddy was mean to his family. That was unfair. Life is not always fair."

I thought about her words for a while, then I turned to face her. "What's my new school like?"

"It will be good. My heart leapt with joy when I heard about it."

"What happened to my eyes, Mom? How did they get this way?"

I wanted to listen and caught a few words—born second, small, trouble breathing, hit your head, pneumonia—all jumbled. I could not hold my head up any longer. The train hummed goodnight with a soft plunk-plunk. I rocked side to side in the big, gray seat and drifted off, wondering how to find courage.

4 DESTINATION

Stops and starts jolted me awake. The train paused to pick up and deliver milk from dairies, which made the eight-hour milk run take longer than it should have. I liked the name milk run because of our dairy, but I was impatient to arrive. When the train moved again, the rail sounds sang. As I became used to the noise, I had to listen hard to hear the clackety-clacks. My comfortable cloth seat began to get tiresome. I stretched and saw Mom watching me with wrinkled brows. She shook her head as if to clear it, dabbed at her cheek, and smiled. She patted my hand, whispered for me to go back to sleep, and promised to wake me later.

I drifted in and out. The darkness passed. Monday turned into Tuesday. I heard her murmur, "Dear God, I promise to write to Gary every week if you will take care of him. Don't let it show how afraid I am. I know I must do this. Thank you for giving us a good place for him."

Uh-oh, I thought. A good place for me? A sour bubble arose in my chest. How does this work?

Dawn's light came through the coach window, and I knew the old rooster at home crowed. I stretched my legs and arms and heard murmuring from other people who wriggled in their seats. Mother smiled and squeezed my hand. The chugging train slowed.

"Son, here's the Alamogordo station."

I had arrived.

5 NMSB – FINGERS AT WORK

The morning after Mom tucked me in, I realized the clicking of her heels on the tiled hallway had not been a nightmare. I warned my roommates not to touch the light switch and stood guard until I followed them out the door. For a week, I would not let anyone touch that black switch on a shiny metal plate hanging halfway up a cream-colored plaster wall. I screamed at anyone who looked ready to dare. I wanted that switch off because that was how she left it.

Maybe that would bring her back. My roommates did not complain about the darkness. Maybe they did not know if the light was on or off. Before long, I learned to give myself a little shock by sliding my feet on the floor and then touching the metal.

Mom flipped that switch on September 5, 1944, the darkest day of my life, and the first night at NMSB. The fancy buildings with roses, the huge shade trees, and the elegant wrought iron fence became my new home. I began to plan my trip back to my family. Mom said I would come for Christmas in three and a half months. I would see her and Dad and Sis and my San Jon farm. I would hear that old rooster crow at dawn. I would clean the chicken coops and the barn, water the pigs, and feed the dogs. I hoped Santa would find me.

Was this a good place to be? I felt lost and by myself with nobody else from San Jon. I was very alone. Homesick day after day. Ten steps from the dining room, I threw up all over the terrace most days and headed straight for my room with a stomach that hurt a lot.

Before I got to NMSB at Alamogordo, I saw a couple of blind men begging on the streets of Tucumcari, the city we shopped in west of San Jon. We put nickels in the beggars' cups, or Dad bought us pencils. I had not been around blind people before that. Every day at Alamo I saw blind grownups and boys and girls. Some could see a little bit, but some could not tell if the sun was bright except by how hot their arms felt. I saw, but not enough to read or write well. Was I like my classmates? My teachers? I couldn't be. Would I be all-the-way blind some day? Would we all be all-the-way blind? I was scared.

At the beginning, I made friends with kindergarten and first grade boys because several lived in the Kindergarten Building with me. There was no lawn grass at home, but at school my friends and I spent a lot of time digging little tunnels in the dry cuttings of the Bermuda grass. We built castles and houses and scenes with the clippings. Best of all, I liked to play on the merry-go-round. We wore sleeved coveralls for outside play. I saw older boys with shirts and overalls without sleeves. I did not know what the girls wore because they played at the other end of the campus. I saw them only in class or chapel when they were in skirts and blouses. We boys wore suits on Sunday, and everyone dressed nicely for study time in my dorm.

The day after I arrived, Mrs. Cole, my classroom teacher, held a tool toward me and asked, "Do you know that reading with fingers started because a three-year-old boy had a terrible accident? Louis lived in France and was playing in his dad's shop. He was using an awl, something like this stylus. It slipped, and he poked his eye out."

My hands flew up to touch my eyes. I felt pain and winced. Poor Louis. His dad made saddles and used an awl to punch holes in the leather.

"My dad won't let me play with an awl. He uses one in our belts and when he fixes our shoes."

"Your father is correct. A bit later, Louis's other eye became infected, and Louis went blind. He could no longer see at all. He was about your age when he left home for a school like this one, a place where he could learn to take care of himself. By the time he was fifteen, Louis thought he would rather die than not read, so he invented a way to write code with dots and he read. Would you like me to show you his code?"

That sounded different. I nodded. The teacher took a sheet of heavy paper, turned it over, and poked it with the sharp tool. I could hear the pokes. "I'm making raised dots and forming patterns," she said, handing the paper to me and guiding my hand.

"Feel this side. It's the back side of the sheet."

It was heavy paper, mostly smooth.

"Turn the paper over, Gary, and feel the front side. What do you feel now?"

"It's bumpy. With little points. They're not all the same. They don't go in a line. Are they in groups?" It was almost scratchy, but the little bumps had not broken the paper, just poked it up.

"Yes, those are the patterns I meant. They stand for letters and punctuation like periods and commas. They also show you if there is a capital letter. Louis moved his fingers over dots. Like this. He knew which patterns meant what and interpreted their meaning with his fingers and his brain. You can learn to read like he did."

Her fingers moved mine, and she continued. "Louis interpreted their meaning as he moved his fingers over the dots. Like this." Mrs. Cole's fingers moved. "Since his name was Louis Braille, they called the code braille. Curiously, to write his code, Louis used an awl, transforming the very implement that took his sight into a useful tool for folks who couldn't see, like some of our teachers and students."

I thought her story and the code intriguing. Maybe I could learn to write to some of the blind kids here. Mrs. Cole told more about Louis Braille and the code. I wondered why she took so long to tell the story. When she said it was time to read, I was surprised, but not in a good way. She refused to give me printed books like I had at my San Jon school. That's when I understood the point of her story. She was talking about me. Sometimes, filled with frustration, I wanted to yell, "Go away and quit bothering me. I can see. Let me have a real book." But I knew I was alone with no one to turn to. My folks were on the farm. I had to get along and do the best I could, so I remained silent.

Then she said, "Gary, let's write your name," and handed me the paper. "Which is the back?"

"Uh, the smooth side, but it's smooth on both sides." I felt like a dummy.

"That's because we have not brailled it yet. I guess I played a little trick on you. When you write, you can start on either side. Once you punch one dot, you have to be sure you are on the correct side of the paper."

I laughed a little but did not feel much better as I began to learn to write braille.

One terrific thing about it was that I was going to be able to read in the dark.

6 DOTS, DOTS, DOTS

I wrote to my parents every two weeks and told everything I could think of—what I was learning, what I was doing, about the boys, how much I tried. It was hard to think of what to say, especially the first time when I did not know that I was going to be telling Mrs. Cole what to write. In each letter, I invited Mom and Dad to visit, but they did not come.

I was ashamed to be throwing up and did not write about that. There were other things I could not tell, not while Mrs. Cole was my scribe. She made me miss play time for small things like being tardy to class or buttoning my shirt incorrectly or for not paying attention. One day when I must have been daydreaming or dropping things, she became very angry.

"Go stand against the wall over there," she said, heading me toward the basement classroom's wall.

I put my back against the concrete and felt panicky while she left me standing for a while. Then she came near and asked brusquely, "You know why you're standing here, don't you?"

With her fingers curled, her hand came up under my chin, thrusting my head back against that cold cement. Bang, bang,

bang several times. I needed an acceptable answer. "I didn't mean to do it" did not work.

I was not the only one treated that way. The other boys and I kept it among ourselves. We told no one else.

Mrs. Cole said she was going to write to Mom and Dad about how I did in September and October 1944. She said my fingers were struggling to talk for me. That was the truth. They did not want to cooperate. She said we could not hurry because my fingers must be my eyes, and that would take a lot of time.

With the way she acted and my stubborn fingers, how long would it take?

"Remember, a braille cell is composed of six dots lined up with two across and three down: number 1 in the upper left corner, number 2 below that in the middle, and 3 at the bottom left; dot 4 in the upper right, 5 at middle right, and 6 in lower right."

I touched the braille model in front of me.

"Each dot or combination of dots makes a letter of the alphabet. A is 1, B is 1 and 2, and the combinations get harder. For instance, W is 2, 4, 5, and 6."

Once again, Mrs. Cole moved my hand along the model to let me be aware of the raised dots. It was hard to feel the code and interpret the letters and numbers. For reading, my left hand was above the paper and at a right angle to my body. My left fingers curved slightly and faced my right hand. My right index finger pointed away from my body and was straight. As my right hand moved from left to right, I felt dots arranged in groups, or patterns, called cells. My left hand also moved along the line, facing my right, and acted as a line keeper. Before my right hand finished the line, my left moved down and found the next line. This was easier than I thought.

As I got faster, I invented a better way. I held my left thumb at a right angle to the paper and read only with it because that thumb was more sensitive. I was pleased to discover an easier way.

"No, no. That is not acceptable," Mrs. Cole said. "Let's start again."

After reading, we practiced writing. For that, I used the stylus to punch the paper from its back side. I turned the page over to read it. In other words, I wrote from right to left and read from left to right.

"You are a brailler," she said.

I was a brailler. Impressive.

The braille slate was made of two pieces of hinged metal, a rectangle eight-and-one-half inches wide and one-and-three-fourth inches high. My slate was used on a standard size paper about eight-and-a-half inches wide and from five to eleven inches tall. I set the slate on my desk with the hinge to the left. I opened it and felt four little points that worked with the hinge to hold the paper securely. I laid the thick paper with the long side snug to the hinge and to the top. When I closed the slate, the points in the bottom piece went into holes in the top piece, anchoring

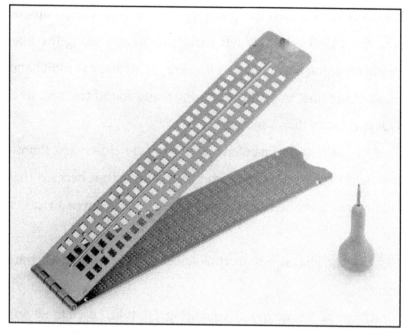

Braille Slate and Stylus,

photo compliments of the American Printing House for the Blind

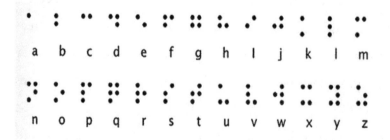

Braille alphabet

my paper. I got all that fine. The problem was I kept forgetting the combinations. I struggled to remember how many dots went where—up, down, or beside.

Horizontally, on the slate's top piece there were cutouts to guide my stylus into the bottom piece's indented six-dotted cells. Those cells were like tiny bowls and stopped the stylus from punching through the paper. We did not want holes, just bumps. A raised horizontal line on the slate kept my place.

How did Louis think of all this stuff? He must have been a genius.

The slate had four lines of cells, so I could write four lines of code on the paper. I made the sharp stylus find the correct indentation to write different letters and numbers, the hard part when I forgot the code. Younger students learned with pegs and a pegboard before they got to use a slate and stylus. More advanced students wrote punctuation marks, symbols, contractions, and even shorthand for whole words. Would I ever do that?

When I was in class, I wrote with the school's braille slate, but soon I spent some of my allowance from home to buy my own slate from the school store. That way, I could practice in my room and write whatever I wanted to.

The teachers were also braillers but had mechanical braille writers. They punched from the bottom and moved up, revealing what had been typed. A person who transcribed written matter into braille was called a braillist. Some of the teachers did that for all-the-way blind people.

On the large tables in the school library, braille books almost twice as thick as my hand was long made me want to read. They were tall and wide, weighing about what Dad's heavy shop hammer weighed. What stories did they tell?

Before I could read them, I had to solve the mystery of all those dots. I wanted to do it before Christmas and show my sister and Mom and Dad something they'd never seen before—reading with fingers instead of eyes.

My mouth pinched up. I chewed my lower lip. I'd have to get much faster. No more thinking about how my life had changed.

7 THE STORE

Mail Call gave me two letters from Mother since I wrote to her, so I knew it was time to say how much I missed her. It was the end of September 1944. I was embarrassed because I felt sorry for myself. The words came tumbling out. The teacher wrote what I said, and I could not stop. I told Mom that I missed my animals and my people and tried not to cry for them. I said I wanted my fingers to do the work but confessed my eyes would peek. I said I hoped to know a few braille letters of the alphabet and write her a letter all by myself because I could spell a great many words. When the teacher told me what to do in the classroom, I tried to do it, but I played outdoors all I could in the wonderful weather. We even had a few days of rain. I made sure to tell Mom that.

I said swimming was fun and thanked her for the last dollar she sent me because I was growing rich. She might send candy. I told her I was looking for it. Sometimes she sent one dollar or gum from an aunt. I took Mom's letters to my room, kissed the envelopes or traced her writing with my finger, and put them in my locker to look at again and again even if I could not read every word.

The most important part of my letter to her said, "Come see me when you can. I will try to learn as much and as fast as I can." I ached for my family to visit and did not want her to know how I suffered with homesickness. She wanted me to get along well at school.

Dad would be happy that I liked shop. Mr. Thomkins was fun and helped me when I made a brush. I told Mom that swimming was scary because I was afraid to get out of the shallow water, but I could go under the water without fear. I asked for a pair of black shoes. My feet were growing fast.

I told Mrs. Cole to write the last part of my letter just the way I said it, "Have you forgotten that I told you to come see me?"

Mrs. Cole said she always wrote what I said, but this time she added that I might start music lessons.

"Really?" I said. "This place is full of surprises."

I wanted to start learning the notes. I must have been doing better because the previous week she told me they did not think it wise to put too many new things upon me all at once, that she thought bowling, gym, shop, swimming, chorus, and braille were plenty, but now she said I would begin violin class in October.

Even with music to look forward to, after dinner I was sick again. I was not able to prevent the vomiting no matter how hard I tried to fight it. Why didn't Mom and Dad come? I wanted them badly. With the war going on, would Dad go to fight the Germans? Maybe they did not want me to know.

Mother wrote back with the exciting news that she and a partner bought the town's only dry goods store. My mother was a shopkeeper and no longer worked for the grocer. I wanted to see the store. She said Dad and Jo Ann helped her clean it because it was a big job. She got rid of high-buttoned shoes and other things out of style to make room for items people wanted to buy, burned them up in a big fire.

I had exciting news, too. When we studied Indians, we built a big tepee, and all ten of us fit inside. We told Indian stories, and I had a break from braille. Mrs. Cole told me she answered Mom's questions. I wondered what Mom had asked. I know she asked how my shoes fit. They fit fine.

I started to think Dad and Mom and Jo Ann were too busy to come. In my Halloween letter I told them not to work too hard. Of course, I was still saying my thoughts out loud to the teacher, but it was a nice letter about the braille slate and stylus I had bought, and I admitted writing was still hard.

"We had two parties for Halloween," I dictated. "On Friday afternoon, we sang songs and played games on the playground with the little kids. Then we went inside the Kindergarten Building and played games with them—Red Rover, Hide and Seek, simple games. If they didn't know how, we taught them."

The big party was even more fun because it was for the whole school.

"We went to the auditorium, and some wore a costume. With kids who could not see, costumes were not as important, but refreshments were. We had red punch and little cookies. Some of the high school boys played instruments, and others told ghost stories. All the ghosts had to stand up and take a bow. The girls sang about a black cat and said mew-mew-mew, and the witches had to take a bow. The senior girls made the auditorium feel scary by moving something that felt like a spider web when it brushed my face. A cook made a little pot of wet, squishy stuff that I did not want to touch because I thought it was worms. We never found out who did it. We played games and got prizes. I won some peanuts."

I wrote so much that it was good I did not have to braille all those words or I would have been there till midnight of the following week.

8   TWINS ASUNDER

My friends and I were not interested in girls or mixing with them at San Jon or NMSB. Jo Ann, my twin sister, was the exception. We played and worked together for eight years. I thought about her, wondered what she was doing, and remembered our skirmishes over toys and heroes, work, and who was right.

We had to watch our language. Mother and Daddy did not want us cussing. Once, when we were little and had not yet started school, we were walking the dusty dirt road along our property carrying cheese and crackers. The way was rutted because there had been a flood a while back.

Sis, always well mannered, stumbled and dropped her food in the dirt. She shouted out, "God Almighty!"

A neighbor called out, "What did you say?"

We had not noticed anyone nearby. Thinking quickly, Jo Ann said, "Got all muddy! Cheese and crackers got all muddy!"

When Dad made me a toy wooden pistol armed with a rubber band, I held the gun up close to my nose and let my fingers explore every part: the solid barrel, the clothespin firing mechanism hooked to the handle, and the rubber-band bullet. The band stretched taut from the tip of the barrel and was held by the spring-operated clothespin. I played with it in the living room the day after he made it and listened to the radio. Sis sat on the divan about six feet away, rustling the pages of her magazines and prattling.

"What makes you think you can listen to Tom Mix? He's no good."

At six, I did not like the way she smarted off. I squeezed the clothespin to let the band fly in her general direction. Who'd have thought I'd get a bullseye?

"Yeow, you hit me on the arm. That hurt. I'll get you for that, Gary Ted Montague," my target said. She grabbed the gun and ran away yelling. I never saw it again.

Mom curled Jo Ann's dark hair around rags every night, and she slept like that. People told Sis she was pretty with her deep dark brown eyes, and she dressed well in skirts made from colorful feed sacks. Dad was real proud of his girl but did not put up with her moods.

When she got angry, Dad would tell her, "Sis, you might as well stop those eyes from snapping when you're mad. You can get un-mad quick as you got mad in the first place."

I bet they were snapping when I hit her with the rubber band, but taking the pistol was retribution enough. She did not tattle.

Another time I was sure they snapped was when I took the crier out of her doll. Sis got mad and started hollering. I told her I wanted to see how it worked, but that time she ran to tell. Daddy chewed me up and spit me out and gave me a licking with his razor strop. I think she was glad. I thought it was worth it.

She did not like me to have Mom to myself on our long day trips to Amarillo, Texas, to see an eye doctor. We rode the bus a hundred miles each way, and we had a lot of waiting at the station and in the doctor's office from the time I was three years old. That's when I got my first glasses. We took that trip every three months until I went to Alamo. Jo Ann did not believe those were long, tiring days, or that my stomach rumbled with hunger and my body ached from sitting still. She acted like I always got everything and begrudged my going on trips.

It was her turn for attention the day everything came to an instant halt in the yard. She cried and screamed, "Something's in my ear. It's moving. It's moving."

I looked in, but she danced around and yowled. I could not see anything. Daddy scooped her up in his arms, and Mom shepherded me straight to the car. We tore out of the place, headed to Tucumcari. She filled the car with noise and tears the whole way. The doctor removed a tick and found no damage to her ear. The critter came from a little lamb she cuddled. Jo Ann was a happy seven-year-old again.

We were together most of the time, but school was our first dividing line because she could see fine. The work was easy for her, so she got ahead of me. She knew better than to tease me about not keeping up. Sometimes I wore an eye patch because the doctor said that might straighten my eyes. She told me some of the boys made fun of me when I was not nearby. She said she did not go along with them because I was her brother, but I knew Mother had warned her she had better not. Everyone liked Jo Ann, and she got along without much trouble, but I listened to be ready to defend her. My first playground fight was with a girl who insulted her. I lost.

When I boarded the train to go to my new school, I was confused about how soon we would be back. Jo Ann and her imaginary friend Jill-Ann-Ann would play together without me there to ignore them. After that, I figured she'd get Dad to take her to the picture show, and they'd get popcorn and maybe ice cream. I loved those. My uncle said she was a Daddy's girl, and that was the truth.

My fraternal twin was named after my mother's favorite hero, Joan of Arc. Mother spelled her name Jo Ann, however, because she was sure one of her school teachers had pronounced the name Jo Ann of Arc. I did not know why Mom and Dad picked my name, but in the 1930s, not many boys in the United States were named Gary, or spear bearer.

Even if we were named after warriors, I had nightmares about how it became impossible for me to protect her. I often woke up praying that God would not let anyone pick on Sis while I was gone.

*Six snapshots show us farming, crops, shovels,
hounds, chickens, pup, and Dad*

Mom made our clothes, homestead

9 RANAHANS AND AROMAS

Dad's smell of cigarette smoke and sweat was gone. Also absent were farm odors: stock, cut hay, leather saddles and harnesses. I missed even cow patties and droppings the animals left behind. They all meant home, but I began forgetting exactly how each one tickled my nose in a different way.

It surprised me that I missed Dad's questions, like "Hey Boy! What'd ya think about this?" He would poke me in the ribs and shove something near my face or triple-poke my arm. Poking was his way. I saw him do that with other cowboys and farmhands. He moved his hands and fingers near a man when he talked.

I had ignored his stories while we worked, but at school I already missed them and wondered what he might say about something I was making or trying to do. He used vocabulary that was different from my new teachers. We would be in the dairy barn getting ready to milk the cows, and he would turn from whatever else he was doing and say, "Guess we'd better get them old ranahans in here and get this milkin' offa hands." By daily repetition, I knew Dad used ranahans or rannies to mean our thirty-eight dairy cows.

I helped drive groups of five or six into the barn and into their stanchions, get the milking machines ready to go, and hook the machines up to the cows' teats. We did it twice a day. I knew he wanted me to help after we finished milking. We would turn the rannies out, clean the equipment, separate the milk from the cream, and put the cans in the ice chest, ready to deliver to the creamery next day.

I was used to his way and understood it. In the Old West, a ranahan was an all-around cowboy at the top of his game, in the middle of all the action. Why he called our dairy cows ranahans, who could say? But I knew when things were done we could go in the house for a meal, and Mom was a great cook.

In my dreams, I heard Mom giggle and saw that shake of her head when she accused Dad of slaughtering the English language. She liked things done proper and that included grammar. At eight, I agreed and knew my new teachers did, too. When I talked like him, I got the feeling Dad's was cowboy talk and not what they wanted to hear from me. He said oglin' or boggin' down the road and must have made up words sometimes. I heard teachers say hurrying or meandering down the road, never an oglin' or boggin'.

A genuine cowboy, my father had a distinguished sounding name, Grant Thomas Montague, but all the grownups called him Tood, rhyming with food.

Our family never had time or money for luxuries beyond going to the picture show, and I always wanted to see who was riding the range. They were handsome like my father. Never heard of a movie cowboy called Tood, but it seemed to suit Dad's speech and manner. Never knew where he got that name, but I noticed he gave a lot of other people nicknames, and they stuck.

I missed my cowboy life. Even Dad's silly games.

He'd tell a little kid, "Hey, see that there? It's a smarter pill. Go git it and eat it."

"No. That's a horse pill. Yuck."

"See? You're gittin' smarter a'ready."

He got a kick out of teasing little kids, but more than likely he'd be telling me, "Go git that shovel." I would look, then feel, for the long handle against a rail or in a corner and hope he had not moved it from where it was last time. He could build anything and had me busy as his helper since I was about six. I pushed my small wheelbarrow or brought the hammer and nails or screws and a driver. He told me what he wanted, and then I moved my hand along the row of boxes or cans to get the right size from the shop.

By the time I was seven, I knew the difference between what went into wood or sheetrock and the kinds of tools we would use. Were they where they were supposed to be, or must I scrunch up my eyes to find them? We had a lot of work to do on the house.

Dad tried to buy a rock house with a tin roof nearer Tucumcari, but he had only enough money for the house nearer San Jon. It had a couple of porches and three rooms. He set about improving it. The floor was wood, covered with linoleum, and the walls were papered wood. Light came through lots of knotholes. Dad cut and flattened Prince Albert tobacco cans.

"Here, Boy, put one of these cans right here so's I can nail it to the outside sheeting."

"One hole covered," I said.

We worked till they were all covered. Afterward, we were tired as rodeo clowns at the end of the show.

"Next we put paper and chicken wire to hold the plaster. You'll like mixin' the plaster, but it takes two coats. We have to let the first coat dry before we start over."

When the outside was done, he repapered the inside. I helped as much as I could, mostly fetching what he needed. It took a spell, but it felt good to be done, and Mom said it looked great. When he had time, we climbed into the old pickup and went to see a neighbor or do a job to earn a few bucks. At my new school in Alamogordo, I spent a lot of time thinking about home.

I missed our tools and how close we stood when we worked. I used to perch on the tongue of the bundle wagon and talk to him. Missed Dad's easy smile, too. But if things did not please him, his mouth was a straight, hard line and he'd get real quiet. I did not miss that.

He got that way when he talked about the war, too. Sometimes he told me what was going on, so I could understand what I saw at the movies or heard President Roosevelt say. The movie newsreel showed action across the pond with our friends, the Allies, and how Germany and Italy and the Japs were fighting us. He told me how hard it was to get new tires and gasoline, and how we all had to do our part and not be greedy.

We did not talk about the war or hard times at school. Everything I knew was gone. Was Dad hurting like I was? Did they miss me when I was not at dinner?

Sometimes I dreamed about the war or Dad or Sis.

10 THE RULE VS. REALITY

I woke up coughing. Hack, hack, hack. Couldn't stop. Tony brought a glass of water.

"You all right?"

"I'm kind of hot and kind of cold," I whispered.

He got Housemother Briggs, who put her hand on my head and said I did not look well. She asked Tony to take me to the infirmary to see Nurse Redding. We walked the short distance, and Tony filled me in about the 15-bed hospital.

"The nurse will give you some medicine and send you back to the room. Once, I was bad sick and stayed overnight, but that doesn't happen most of the time."

About halfway across the campus, between the Kindergarten and the Junior-Senior Dorms, stood a small one-story brick building I had never been in. I felt worse and was glad there was only one step up. Tony stopped. I reached for the doorframe. My nose twitched, and I hesitated at the antiseptic smell, then stepped into a well-lit white room. The floor was tiled, like in my building.

Nurse Redding wore white. After Tony hurried off to chapel, she took me into her office across from the entrance. As she spoke in a soft, clear, reassuring voice, I knew she cared about me and took me seriously.

"Here's my special cough medicine, my secret formula. It will fix you right up. It's bitter, but it works. Open up."

I swallowed the vinegary liquid and lay down in the boys' side of the infirmary. A girl must have been sick in a bed at the girls' end because soon I heard someone talking softly.

Later, Nurse Redding told me, "That one over there is going to have to stay for a while. She'll be here overnight. If you ever get real sick, we'll take you downtown to Dr. Simms. He's a busy man, so he comes out only once a week to check on the types of medicines we need. I take care of everything else, like cuts and scrapes—and coughs." She sat by the bed and told me about the life she had in South America when she was young and wanted adventure.

"Do you speak Spanish?" I asked.

"Yes, but I use English here."

"I do, too."

The nurse continued, "You tell your housemother I said for you to take it easy today, but you can go to class tomorrow. I want you to play quietly and not run around much. You can't rest long, though, because you'll have to make up all the work you miss. Come back if your cough doesn't go away."

My new friend made me happy. Her formula was super special, and I got well fast. I began to spend more time in the infirmary. She had other medicines, like tetracycline for the flu.

The warm fall turned cooler. Leaves fell to crunch underfoot as I walked toward refuge with Nurse Redding. When I was homesick, she made me feel more courageous. I liked learning from her because she was full of ideas.

It was good for me when I moved to the Junior Building with older boys, all eleven to fourteen. I had not lived with the babies very long. They had not been bad, but we did not care for the same things, and I wanted to be with older boys.

The room and locker were a scant larger. I did not have many personal possessions except for my clothes and letters. Pancho, Tony, David, and I had a pact to be brothers. They all spoke Spanish at home, and sometimes lined up against me, but they did not make me feel stupid most of the time.

The greatest challenge about NMSB was that only three or four other kids out of the eighty to ninety students spoke English when teachers or housemothers were not around. That made me feel like I did not belong. The teachers said we were supposed to speak English all the time, but when the grownups were not listening, the boys used Spanish, and I guess the girls did, too. I started to understand what they were saying, but the teachers made us sit on chairs in our bedrooms if they caught us speaking Spanish. It did not seem fair, and none of us liked being stuck alone in our rooms.

Learning to speak a new language at the same time as learning braille codes for reading and writing challenged my mind. I wanted to know how everything around me was made, how it worked, and how it fit together. Mr. Thomkins called that a system. My fingers traced edges and changes in surfaces, explored bracing, took items apart, and put them back together. Sometimes my friends called me Mr. Curious.

While that was friendly teasing, I could not predict how other boys would treat me physically. I was the butt of bullying both on and off the playground, but I did not want to look like a weakling. Most incidents in the dining room and my building were mild because adults were present, and we were good kids. All I wanted to do was get along and help everybody.

Ever since my first week at the school, I had had problems because I did not know what some boys meant when they whispered under their breaths or called me names in Spanish while we waited in line. They said *ciego* (blind one), *terreno* (one encroaching in someone's space), *tuerto* (cross-eyed, one-eyed, blind in one eye), *retorcido* (twisted), *terco* (pig-headed), or *gabacho* or *gringo* (Anglo). It was ironic that some of their words described themselves, but I was learning the culture of the blind.

The names were put-downs. I thought the boys were being mean and called them whatever I could think of in English. Boy stuff, but no less stinging. The terms got louder and more negative outside the classroom. I understood their tone and implications and felt out of place before I could translate their nasty slang. I got mad or had a case of the "sorrys."

Upset boys often reacted with their fists, even for an accidental bump or a word taken wrong. They made up stories just to see what the victim would do, anything to get a fight started. Sometimes I became the target of their derision. Hating bullies but being stubborn, I did the same. There was a code of silence, a strict unwritten rule that there was no tattling to adults. Because I saw better than many of the others, I should have had an advantage; but I was also inexperienced in fist fighting.

One thing about it, I began to learn a little Spanish and a lot about fighting.

Daydreams about home, where I knew what was what and where nobody spoke a different language, always kept me company because I had a useful place there. I was an important part of the family. At school, I remained confused about how I fit in with all the people trying to look after me. At home, even when we got mad, we stuck together.

Was my sister thinking about me, or was she dreaming of movie and soap opera stars?

11 BIG PLANS

It was November 21, 1944, and I dreamt of turkey and dressing, gravy and cranberry sauce, and pumpkin pie. Time to write home with Thanksgiving greetings.

"I will eat a big dinner and play all afternoon. I will have to go to school on Friday. Will Jo Ann have a holiday?" Mrs. Cole wrote for me.

"Does Jo Ann get gold stars like last year? Mrs. Cole will give a prize to the one who earns the most stars, but I won't get it this time because I'm still not doing too well with my braille reading and writing. I am doing better, and I have earned eight stars, and that shows I am trying. I promise to do more. I'll try to win the prize next time."

"I'm sure you'll get a prize when you let your fingers read and write for you," Mrs. Cole said. "Keep trying to do your best. What else do you want to tell your mother and father?"

I wrote about the music we would skate to at a party this coming Saturday. I expected lots of fun because we would have booths to buy candy, cookies, and pop. It would be like a real carnival. I asked if Jo Ann saw *Snow White and the Seven Dwarfs* and told them how I liked Doc the best and enjoyed the movie. I explained how we set up the Pilgrim story on our sand table and had Indians, pilgrims, trees, cabins, squirrels, and turkeys. It told a real story. The Mayflower stood in the background.

"How do you want to end your letter, Gary?"

"Thank you for all the money and nice letters you have sent me. The cookies did not last long. Love to all."

During playtime, we roller-skated for fun, but we stayed on the sidewalks near our own dorms because boys and girls were not allowed to play together. I had a special key to tighten my skates onto my shoes. In my next letter, I told about going fast along the big loop of concrete near the administration building. The party was on a cold day. I fell a few times, but it did not hurt, and I had a good time, especially since some boys and girls came from town to skate with us. I used allowance money to buy cookies and candy and shared with one of the boys.

There was more to say because by the end of November I could read some braille and could almost write my long name, even though it was hard. I also liked playing the violin and knew "Jingle Bells." I asked them to send my dump truck if Dad had fixed it and not to forget to come after me for Christmas.

"Just a few more weeks now, and I will see you again. Write to me soon."

I was excited when Christmas activities started. Our choruses sang together like a big family instead of by age. I was learning carols with the Senior Chorus. We would have a program for the public in about five days. I wrote about it in the middle of

December to give my parents enough time to plan for their visit. It was Friday, and the concert would be the last event before I went home.

"I wish you could hear us. We are going to have Christmas trees in all the buildings. Decorations will be up by Saturday. Don't forget me. I will be so glad to see you."

Teacher also wrote a personal letter to them.

"Gary, I told Mom and Dad that you read braille and write a little, too. We can send them a few of your sentences. I said you are anxious to show them how, so I'll let you take a book home. Remember not to read it with your eyes. You know, Gary, you can learn it if you concentrate. I know it is not easy for you yet, but you have made marked improvement. I hope they are pleased when they see what you can do."

"I can read whole sentences, and I like when I do that," I said.

"Yes, it takes a lot of time, but you are persistent and try hard. You will master written braille. I told them to be sure to send you back to us after having a good Christmas."

I made big plans in my dorm room. I sang right out loud. Chill bumps of joy made me shiver. I danced and sang.

Christmas is coming, and I'll be packing,

going home, home,

home on the range

to Sis, Mom, and Dad, and the animals,

Mom's cooking, Santa Claus, and

all the decorations,

red, green, and gold.

By myself I'll go on the train,

on the train,

My dogs are barking and waiting

to sing hello!

I wanted to smell Dad and be around him and his tools when he called "Ted!" and I knew to come immediately. Lots of my relatives called me Ted or Gary Ted.

I wanted to eat Mom's delicious fried chicken and her homemade chocolate syrup on pancakes. She could say, "Now, Gary," and waggle her right index finger to scold me, and I would not mind.

Putting my thoughts to a beat, I added a few tra-la-las. I held onto a note or sang words with a lilting click-click-clickety-click, whatever fit the moment. Put to a tune, that made a pretty good song.

Dad's beef's best in the world,

and Mother beats batter for cake,

tall dark chocolate cake

with thick fudge icing.

I'll have them soon. Yum!

Coconut bonbons dipped in chocolate.

Eagle Brand pudding.

Special Christmas treats

waiting for me.

With an abrupt pause, I yelled, "If I'd a-known I would live at this new school forever, I wouldn't of got on that train."

Out came the great big rawhide suitcase. I packed for my first trip alone. My roommates packed their bags and joined me in a few tra-la-las and the fun of singing and anticipating what we would do on our vacation. A couple of the boys had been at school longer than I, so this was not their first experience, but I had never had a going-home vacation like this before. All of us were laughing and telling what fascinating things we would do.

12 HOME FOR CHRISTMAS

The ride home was terrific. This time there was no freight, so the engineer let me wear his cap while we walked all the way to the caboose and forward to the engineer's cab. He showed me the throttle, the air-brake controls, the sand controls, and several gauges and indicators that told the engineer and his assistant, the fireman, how well the locomotive was performing. The brakeman and conductor visited with me, too. I arrived at the Tucumcari depot in a very good mood. Dad stood by the pickup with a broad grin on his welcoming face.

At our house, I peeked inside every little canister and jar with a lid. Some had narrow red ribbons around their necks and small sprigs of green. All kinds of mouth-watering smells hinted of tastiness. Jo Ann told me that for weeks Mom held back on the rationed sugar to have enough to send me goodies and make holiday cookies, date loaf, Brazil nut fruitcake, English toffee, and those little coconut candies dipped in chocolate. Rationing was the way it was during World War II. Everything was decorated and delicious.

"You did a good job, Sis. Want to play some games?"

"I've got a new comic book I can read to you," she replied.

Since I had trouble making sense of the pictures, I seldom looked at any kind of funnies, but she made it interesting before we played the games.

Outside, my dogs jumped on me and wagged their whole back ends with joy each time they smelled my scent and heard my voice. They sniffed me all over, and I laughed when I pushed them away. They came back for more. We played hard out near the fields and the barn and corrals. I ran my hands down their backs and scratched behind their ears. We checked out the hens and cattle, the pigs and horses.

"Hey, Dad, you got the place looking good."

"Boy, I saved some repairs fer you to help me with."

His tools felt good in my hands. I squeezed the handles and rolled them in my palms, balancing and regripping. I had dreamed of them and how I'd make sure they got back where they belonged. We braced up a couple of shelves in the barn and resoled one of my shoes. I found Dad's awl and told him about Louis and the stylus.

A few days before Christmas, I saw the postmistress, Mrs. Holly, when I went for the morning mail. She acted like she'd missed me.

"I hear it's real nice down there in Alamogordo. Your mom thought the buildings and flowers looked good when she was there. People were friendly to her, too. She thought the Christmas decorations must look real pretty, with colored lights and red balls on the trees. She wished she could see them and hear your public performance."

"I asked her to come," I said. "I wanted her to come."

"The teacher..."

My forehead wrinkled, and my head jerked. Had I heard Mrs. Holly say something about my teacher? A big family came in, and I missed some of her words. By the time I could ask Mom, she said something about having lots of work to do and not a thing about my teacher, so I forgot.

"How come you bought this store, Mom? Do you like working here better than in Shorty's grocery store?"

"Son, I love being the proprietor of my own business. Ola Naylor, you remember she's married to Alvin with the big ranch? She's a wonderful partner. She works as hard as I do."

Mother sold the cotton crochet thread and fabrics she loved. She had cowboy hats and boots, coveralls and work boots, ladies' dresses and bonnets, lots of other clothing, sheets and towels, and gift items. The days demanded a lot from her but improved family finances. She paid the bills when due.

The metal cash register fascinated me. I liked to rub my fingers over it because there were curlicues and designs. A bell pinged each time I opened it. I also learned how to shelve. We would have to shop in Tucumcari for me because she did not carry my size yet.

San Jon Dry Goods closed for Christmas Eve because it was Sunday. We also closed for Christmas Day and the day after. We drove about three hours to Grandmother Moore's at Happy, Texas, to have a big dinner with Mom's family. The smell was tantalizing. The tables had smooth, damask tablecloths and crystal candlesticks. All the sisters had brought their best dishes and utensils to make it a fine celebration. A big turkey was the main course.

Granddad Moore stayed in his room because he was bedridden, which was fine with me because he did not believe in Christmas like the rest of us. In honor of the baby Jesus, I tried to be nice and not to trick Granddad when I adjusted his radio. I usually messed it up on purpose because Mom told me he had been mean to his family. When she was growing up, he made Christmas an ordinary work day even though he had tried to beat religion into his children. The rest of us adored Christmas and the beauty of the Nativity story.

Aunt Florence gave a long prayer about being thankful for Jesus and that we were together, including me, and please for the Lord to take care of her brothers wherever they were because they were protecting us. She listed each by name: Doc, Wheeler, Luther, and Liston. Mom and Aunts Florence, Wanda, and Ethel, served a delicious dinner and talked about needlework, food shortages, and rationing. We opened presents and played games. Uncle Red told stories. Grandmother Moore asked about school. I read to her from my braille book. My cousins, Valmore and Irene, were much older than Jo Ann and I, and they brought us home-knit sweaters. The men smoked and laughed. They talked about hard times, horses, and how the President was doing with the war. They relived the liberation of Paris and told what they knew about Mom's brothers fighting the Nazis and the Japanese. Our celebration ended a little after sunset, and we headed home.

"Dad, how'd the war start? Did the damn Japs really drop bombs on our ships?"

"Son, watch what you say," Mom corrected.

"That's what somebody said."

"He may have, but you do not talk that way."

"Sorry, Mom. But is it true about the bombs?"

Dad told how shocked he was a couple of weeks before Christmas when I was five. I learned about Pearl Harbor and how Hawaii was in the Pacific Ocean. He called it Hi-wah-ya. Mom said the German Nazis were in another part of the world, in Europe, and it was a land war. Our soldiers had to go across the Atlantic Ocean to get there. They were fighting for freedom.

Sis and I fell asleep on the ride home. It was the best day I'd had in a long time.

A few days after Christmas, while Mom stocked shelves, her customer, Mrs. Roberts, told me how glad my family had been that I would be coming home. She was full of details and ideas that tumbled over one another in her conversation. I could hardly keep up or say much. She asked about my vacation, but not about what I did while I was gone.

"Your mother was sure you'd want to see the store and spend time here when you came home for Christmas. She said you would look at every little thing and check out the merchandise, and that you'd probably examine the shelves and how the cash register works. Did you go over to Texas to see the Moore family?"

"Yes, we did. I saw my grandparents and aunts and uncles and cousins at a big dinner. We had to hurry to get back to the animals and the store."

"It's too bad you missed harvest and the Quay County Rodeo this fall. My, my, you're such a big boy to come home on the train all by yourself. Did Hazel have something special for you when you arrived?"

"Yes, ma'am. A big fudge cake. It was so good."

"We-ell." She pronounced it as if it were two syllables. "That's what she said she'd do. I like that thick fudge icing she makes with a tiny bit of coffee in it. She really was ready for you to be here, Gary Ted. Did you find a peculiar-looking package under your tree by any chance?"

"My violin! You know about my violin?"

Mom's talkative friend gave a deep chuckle that shifted her heavy weight, so I thought it was a real knee slapper and laughed too. I was so glad to be home.

"I stood right here while she wrapped that odd shape in the prettiest red paper she had in the store. Put a fresh-tied bow of scarlet satin on it, too." Her fingers stroked the reel of wide red ribbon on the counter.

"You know, she's an expert at tying great big bows and loves red. It wasn't easy to wrap, but she's good at that. Hazel told me how excited she was about that little violin. It's half-size so's it fits your hands. Your whole family went together and raised thirty dollars to buy that for you. Better take good care of it and learn to play."

"For sure. That's a lot of money. I didn't know it cost that much. I borrowed one at school, but my teacher's going to teach me to play this one, and I'll take real good care of it. Don't you worry about that."

"Mr. Tood was anxious to see you, too."

"I know. He told me he was curious about what I'd learned."

"He could hardly bear it when you got on that train to go down there."

About that time, Mom came around the counter and rescued me from Mrs. Talk-Talk. "I don't understand how three months can feel like so much longer. Seemed like he was a thousand miles away, but it's only three hundred. Son, would you mind going for the afternoon mail?"

On my way to the post office, I got so caught up scuffing my cowboy boots in the light snow on the sidewalk that I did not think about Postmistress Holly or Mrs. Talk-Talk till much later.

One of the best parts of my wonderful Christmas visit was when I read from braille magazines, and Mom and Dad kept trying to turn up the kerosene lamp. Sis got extra mad when I read under the covers because she could not. None of them figured out how this worked!

Too soon, though, we were back aboard the Southern Pacific, Mom, me, and my special violin.

13 MUSIC AND MORE LETTERS

January nights were cold, so my friend Lucio and I came in from the dining hall, pulled off our light jackets, finished homework, and played a game of checkers. The end of school was a whole month closer because the following day would be February. I was going to have so much fun this summer and already had plans.

"At Christmas, I told my dogs and horses I'd see them soon," I told Lucio.

"What do you call them?"

"Old Blue's the hound. My horses are Ball-ee, and Zephyr. I bet they're waiting for me right now. They don't mind the cold."

"It's colder in Santa Fe than here. My folks have snow. I wish we had snow. Did you ever build a snowman?"

I nodded.

"My brother says they had so much snow that he rolled a huge stomach so big it took three boys to put it up where it belonged."

Lucio rounded his arms and held them out in front of him with a big toothy grin. His eyes opened wide. I figured it was one of his tall tales.

I said, "Jo Ann and I had so much wet stuff we built a snowman and a snowcow but had trouble milking her."

We roared in laughter. It felt good. I moved a red checker. He saw a little better than I did, but our wins were the same. I kept thinking of what I would carry on the train when I went home next summer. Maybe I would make a little brush or a basket in shop class and put it inside the rawhide suitcase. Mom and Dad would be proud of me. Jo Ann would read her books out loud in the days, and I would read braille magazines at night.

I told Lucio, "I wish I could leave for home now. Maybe they will come soon. If I could drive, I'd find an old pickup, throw my stuff in quicker than anything, and make short work of those 300 miles, singing Old Black Joe, first the melody, then my part, then the melody, all the way while the miles flew by. You could come with me and play the violin."

"I could help you drive. Your mom would fix me fried chicken and chocolate cake."

"Then you could drive to Santa Fe."

We roared again. I missed a move, and Lucio's king checkmated me. It was bedtime.

The days had flown through January, except in writing class. When I finished reading my first volume of braille with Mrs. Cole, it was a great day. I believed I did not need to be writing with a stylus or using an apron over my hands. Dots, dots, so many stubborn dots. And my teacher was picky. When I was home, I looked at some of Jo Ann's writing and could tell what the letters were. I traced over them. Sis was quick with her pencil. These confounded dots were hard to punch in the right order. I went extra slow, so they would be right and I would not need to begin again. At least, I could braille all my numbers.

"Gary Montague, what are you doing? Think. Try. Are you daydreaming?" Mrs. Cole's voice interrupted my thoughts. I jumped a bit and did not care if I ever wrote my own letters. Nobody would hear from me. That would show her.

But she would not let that be. Before I would get on the train, she would make me write seven more letters, two each for February, March, and April and one in May. I knew she would because she told me to write two a month ever since I arrived. Mrs. Cole always said my writing was not good enough, no matter how careful I was. Mom would be ashamed of me if I refused to do it. My job was to go to school and try hard. That's what I did.

Maybe we would have a party to celebrate if I ever wrote my own letter.

I liked the party the previous week. Big Bingo cards with both braille and printed letters let everyone play. Because Bobby and Edward had the mumps, I tried to stay out of the hospital, but I saved a little candy for them because they did not get to come.

"Gary, come play a game with me," Mrs. Cole said at the party. I could not say no. Maybe she would like me better, so I did. It was fun.

Then Mrs. Cole told everyone, "Juanita is the winner of the Guess the Number of Peanuts in the Jar." She gave the girl a prize. "Dickie has won a prize for having the lucky ticket."

Maybe I would get a prize next time. We all bought candy, cookies, and Cokes. I used some of the $2 Mom sent every month.

Besides parties, I liked shop class and Mom's packages of sweets. I got a sweater, new pants, and a shirt, too. I was happy January was over. I was trying to learn to swim. Most days, I was not afraid of the water.

Some of the best fun was in violin class with Miss Clark. It was a lot of work, but I liked the other three boys in the violin orchestra. Macario, David, and Lucio performed as a trio last week. They were a couple of years older than I. Miss Clark said I was good enough to make it a quartet. We each had our own practice times outside of class.

She told us, "Boys, I am watching your strokes very closely. Don't be nervous. I will make sure your bows rise and fall at the same time so that your sound is good."

Like them, I held my bow as Miss Clark adjusted each of them. The hair had to be just so, and so did our fingers.

"Put your fingers like this. Try to sense what your fingers feel."

I held the fiddle under my chin. She put her hand on mine to show how to hold the bow and how tightly it had to be drawn to make it sound right.

"Place your little finger between the bow back and the bow hair and tighten the knurled knob at the back end of the bow," Miss Clark said. "The thickness of your little finger is the proper distance between the hair and back."

I did not want anything but the bow hair to strike the strings because it would not sound right and might damage the bow or the violin. Loose bow hair sounded scratchy. I adjusted the tension.

"Listen for the tone." I heard Miss Clark's tuner or a note on the piano. She taught me to tune the catgut strings of my instrument. I loved it.

I told Mom and Dad about the parties, swimming, and violin in my Valentine letter, but there was so much I wanted to say and could not fit in. We had another party and a Valentine's box in our classroom. Mrs. Cole told us to make cards for each other and one to send home. I did not use my head and made mine too large. Why didn't I do it right? I wanted Mom and Dad to know I loved them in a big way, but it was too big to mail. I told them I loved them and was looking for Mom's Valentine's candy that had not arrived.

The day was wonderful, even without her package, and I went to two more parties. Kindergarten invited us to play games, swim, and have pop and cookies. Then we listened to second grade read an Eskimo story. We talked about the Northland and made an Eskimo village from paper and clay. We told stories and wrote them. Mine was good. I wrote four sentences and sent my story home. They would see I did not give up.

Candy and valentines came from Uncle Wheeler and Uncle Luther. I went to bed wondering why I did not hear from Mom. I always thanked her. Her letters were good. How could she forget Valentine's?

I tasted her chocolates in my dreams until a box finally came the following morning with a letter. Mom said she went to see Grandma. I wanted to see her, too.

I dictated the next letter a couple of weeks later. It was the week after Washington's birthday. I told Mother it was nice to know she still loved me and asked for a checkerboard and checkers.

I wondered how the war was going, but we did not listen to the President's *Fireside Chats* at school as we had on the home radio, so I did not tell Mrs. Cole to put that in my letter.

At the party with Cub Scouts from school and from town, I found out their master was a soldier who was transferred. I wondered if he went to war. No one said, but their new master was a sergeant. I heard him say something about an island, Eewo-something. He acted happy, so I think we had a victory. The teachers did not tell us about the war in class. I wondered how our soldiers were doing, if my uncles were safe, and if Dad would go.

The sergeant said, "How old are you, Gary?"

"I'll be old enough to be a Cub next year, Sir. I'll be glad because they have a lot of fun."

"We'll look for you next time we come," he said.

"The Cubs in our classroom put on a play for Lincoln's birthday. Mrs. Cole helped them. I wanted to be up there."

My voice sounded funny because I cheered so loud for our older boys who wrestled in a tournament the previous day. We boys on the sidelines liked yelling with the girls who led the cheering squad and jumped around the floor of the auditorium. It was a lot more interesting than braille. I thought I might wrestle someday.

Violin got even better when Valentino made us into a quintet. He was my good friend, but he had a bad arm. Miss Clark told him he could play just as well as we did.

"Gary, you and Valentino are working well on 'A Cradle Song,' so I am giving you a piece with open strings. You will pluck the strings with your fingers. Let me show you."

I was hesitant, but she knew how to build my confidence fast. I looked at her and thought of Mom. They were about the same size with dark brown hair, glasses, and a gentle manner. Other teachers told me they looked alike. Both were firm, but not in a bad way.

My mother and Miss Clark were different from Mrs. Cole, who read good stories about Eskimos and Shoshones but would not let me count on my fingers while I learned my facts.

"What if your fingers got cut off and you needed to know how much something cost? What if they froze, and you could not move them?" she asked.

Thinking fast was good. I liked it, but sometimes I could not think.

"No matter how old you get, nine plus seven will always be sixteen," she said. "Gary, I see you are happy and very busy. Please don't feel badly about your writing. In time, it will come. Your fingers don't always cooperate, but we know how to train them. You will improve if you are patient."

I did not know how to answer. "All right," I said.

I was glad when playtime came.

14 SUMMER NEARS

I dictated the March letter exactly two months before my birthday. Surely, I would be allowed to write my own letter home next time, and I would make it perfect. I hoped to go home soon, home where I would work hard with my wagon and finish filling a big hole. I thought about going a lot. I was almost finished with a brush more than a half foot long. It was for Mom. Then I'd make a bigger one for Dad.

I hummed the prayer response and a hymn I was learning. I wished I could put my voice in the envelope.

"Gary, back to your letter," Mrs. Cole said. "What else do you want to tell your mom and dad? What about your sister?"

"I run and jump into the warm water in the pool and will be a good swimmer—did I tell them about the track team?"

"What about track?"

"The boys have a track and field team. The gym teacher wanted me to join, but I didn't, and now I'm sorry as they do have lots of fun and learn a lot, too."

My mind churned till I thought of my new reading book.

"I am going to read four pages in braille for each lesson. At first, I could read only a line or two, then a page, and now four.

The pages are not very long and quite easy, and the end of a sentence might be on the next page. I want to finish by the end of the month."

Mrs. Cole looked at me. "Anything about arithmetic?"

"I do not count with my fingers."

Mrs. Cole patted my hand. "Your oral arithmetic, spelling, and English are far beyond your reading and writing. Your mind thinks fast. When your fingers develop the touch, you will go like lightning. Let's both be patient."

A farm crop took a long time to mature and be ready to harvest. Were my fingers like that? Like little chicks growing inside their shells? If you tried to help them out, they would die. How long was I supposed to wait?

One day, when the teacher told me there were only five weeks left in the school year, I was happy. I worked at writing better when I was not busy with something else. I counted the days till school would end. I told Mom and Dad how much better I was getting when I dictated my April letter.

The hard wind and no rain made my cold bad, but I told Jo Ann I could go to Cub Scout meetings as a guest, even with a cold. It was for boys, so I knew I could not take her with me if she lived in Alamogordo. She probably would prefer to be with girls and do girl things, like sew and talk about movie stars. I thanked Mom for the gum.

That pesky braille kept giving me grief. Why were my hands

and fingers awkward no matter how much I wanted to control them and put those little dots in their cells?

"You do not try hard enough, Gary. You know all your letters and can spell the words. It's time for you to put them on braille paper."

I did think. I did try. I got flustered. She never was satisfied. I was tired of telling her what I wanted to say. My eyes stung with tears no one was ever going to see. Relief would come with the whole summer at home on the farm where people were not fussy and mean, and things were not so hard.

For now, I twisted my thinking to say the right things.

"Oh, my!" I dictated to Mrs. Cole. "I hope you had a nice time visiting Grandpa. I would like to have been with you. We had good activities the past two weeks. The Home Ec girls gave a style show Friday night. It was crowded because the public attended. The girls sewed their own dresses."

"What about the boys?"

"On Saturday before last, a group of us had a fun picnic out at White Sands. I took off my shoes and socks and felt sharp grit between my toes and stuck to my soles. It was bright white, not like the sand at home. It was so white I wanted to shut my eyes. We stayed on one huge dune. It was too soft for us to run around without sinking or tumbling. Did you ever see sand white as snow? We saw lots and lots of it, and we had to stick together. I can take you there when you come."

I told how the Athletic Association went on another day, but I could not be in that club until I was twelve. That I could be a real Cub Scout next year. That my cold was better, but I could not swim last week.

I knew I was racing to get done until I thought of something so important and happy that I had to have Mrs. Cole write about it.

"Isn't the war news from Germany exciting? We went to the movies and watched a newsreel about the Allies defeating the Germans and freeing prisoners. How are my uncles? Are they in Germany? I hope we win."

"Anything else?"

"Yes. I want to tell them about the photographers."

"Go ahead."

I told how busy it was for our teachers because so many visitors had come to watch us work and play. A photographer from Albuquerque took pictures in my classroom. He had a big flashgun. We had to sit very still.

"I try to write letters like yours, Mother. Thank you for the shoes and all the packages this year. I send my love and shall be so glad to see you. It's not long till I shall be home."

I would not have seven letters to write, after all. Time was short. I was ready. My fingers twitched at the thought. They moved fast. Maybe that's why the braille was hard. Maybe they did not want to go slow.

My ninth birthday was two days earlier. That meant I was

one week from home. I prayed, "God, please keep Mom and Dad, Sis, and me safe."

I tried to remember what Mrs. Cole read from the report she was sending to my parents. She used a lot of words I forgot, except she said I was bright and intelligent and would make all my grades easily once I mastered braille. Since I knew the codes but needed practice, she was sending a braille reading book and a slate and paper with me. Humph. Summer homework. Maybe Jo Ann would do some of it.

I prayed again, "Dear God, please don't let my dog or horse run off. Keep all of us well and happy till I get home."

Mrs. Cole also had said I adjusted well to the school, but she did not give me any new gold stars or say I did good.

The other thing I remembered was that I would be listed as a special student in this school with work in grades two and three until braille became easier for me. I was listening for fourth grade, but it was not there. The rest was confusing, but I got the part about the braille and knew I was not going to fourth grade. I did not ask her what the rest meant.

The train would take me home all by myself on Saturday. Mother would bake a chocolate birthday cake with thick fudge icing and candles. I made more plans, brandings and farming and building stuff with Dad.

Jo Ann would have a new teacher next year. Would I?

15 SUMMER NORMALCY

I patted my jeans and felt a hard lump with my pocket knife where it belonged. Chores felt right, too. I was ready for building and branding and volunteered to clean. I pulled out my knife, opened it, stared at the single blade to be sure there were no nicks. Swiped, swiped, swiped on my Dickies. I smiled and closed it with a snap. I put it in the pocket on my right side where it rubbed against my thigh. A man ought to have his knife with him all the time in case he needs to dig something out, cut a string, or shave wood. It did not look like anyone had messed with it while I was gone.

I found my pouch of marbles at the back of the drawer where I left it. I had played at San Jon but not at Alamo. How many did I have? I started by the big elm, but the ground was tilted so they rolled. The shade obscured my view, and I lost a couple.

Old Blue came loping over, never minding where he stepped. "Get down, Blue, you got my face wet. Watch it."

We moved over by the kitchen. "Sit, Blue." I cleared a space, brushed it with my hands and tamped dirt with my feet but still had trouble. I filled my wagon with small rocks and short sticks and made a circle near the back door. Blue lost interest and wandered off. I shot marbles in my little arena. That worked well until bigger feet came home and knocked some of it aside.

"You got to move that, Gary, before I trip."

I moved it again. Mom shot a few with me, then Dad tried. They sure could aim.

Life was normal when I got back to the animals and went to brandings with Dad. I liked sleeping on the porch. The outhouse was a different story. Each of us poured lime from a bucket into the hole to control odors and germs. No one wanted to do it, but Jo Ann acted disgusted and considered it a major chore. Mother or Daddy always made sure there were plenty of Sears or Montgomery Ward catalog pages to use out there because we did not have toilet paper.

I was an energetic nine-year-old kid with lots of freedom to explore the fields and pastures, the barn, and the well house. No more throwing up. Mom and Sis were in town at our store. Dad worked for other ranchers or widows. Being alone at the farm was not the same as loneliness at school because animals kept me company. I wished I could see the arch in a cat's back or his hair standing up, warning me to stay away. I played with the dogs and used trial and error to discover a few rules of nature without seeing the signs:

- Listen to cattle bawling or making various sounds to know when they want food or appreciate being patted or rubbed.

- Pay attention when dogs bark or nudge my hand because some are friendly and sense things are not the same with me as with others. They stay nearby and bark to protect me. Watch out for temperamental ones.
- Keep my hand out of holes because snakes, rats, or other carnivorous varmints might be in there.
- Run after farm cats or chickens all I want but know they do not like to be held.
- Approach cows and horses from the front, or they might kick or step on me.
- Enjoy staring at pigs, but they do not like to be messed with and are very dirty. They squeal or bite.
- Sheep and goats are unpredictable. Sheep rub against me, knocking me over. Goats butt me or climb on something and jump me. Avoid both.
- Never get between any animals and their food.
- Notice a trembling horse because he might announce a storm or a snake or the presence of a predator.
- Cats overturn milk buckets.

When Dad was with me, I imitated his work with the horses. I stroked a horse's body for alerts before placing a blanket or saddle on his back. I was annoyed at not being able to see what the horse was doing so I could anticipate change. A horse with bared teeth might paw or kick me. I depended on hearing forepaws scraping the ground or too much inhaling as a warning to react quickly, like the day with Old Zephyr. My hands held the reins and his bridle.

"Come on, Zeph, let's go to the field."

I heard him paw the ground and inhale. I let go and ran in another direction. He was easy to get along with, but that day he had a mind of his own.

I paid attention to messages my hands felt on the reins and started to pick up on other cues quicker. I practiced riding, too. Dad was nearby when I worked with the horses, but I felt like I was doing it alone.

My chest swelled with pride when he said, "Boy, you're a durn good rider, better'n when you first got back here. A savvy cowboy."

Relationships and timing were important when I followed his directions. He explained how things worked, such as where to place the saddle on a horse's back, how tight the cinch must be, how to put on a bridle, and what kind of bridle to use to make the horse do what I wanted. Bridles with steel bits could make a horse's mouth sore.

"Use a hackamore, Boy. It's a halter that uses a metal piece under Zephyr's chin so when you pull, your horse stops without getting a sore mouth."

"I don't want to hurt him. I'll remember."

I wished my eyes could warn me in time to avoid deep holes, a protrusion, or an object's sharpness. When Mother took Sis, me, and some other kids out to the Adams' farm where there was an oversized metal stock tank we could swim in, we ran toward the cool water.

"Yeow!" Burning bloody scratches lined my legs and arms. Mom and I nursed my wounds, and I did not splash with the others because I had not seen the barbed wire fence. I could not show I knew how to swim.

My eyes frustrated Dad, and he made me feel like I was never good enough. I heard a lot of "Pay attention!" "Look here, Boy." "Watch me."

Look where?

"Do it this way."

How? How do I hold my fingers? I strained to see, but he had moved to the next step. I was not inattentive. He was hard to follow. I wanted a little peace, to get along, and to do a good job without disappointing either of us.

Dad's work began just before the sun came up, required him to figure out how to fix problems, and stopped when the sun went down. He considered me his helper, his ranahan who should not need much instruction to keep up. Mom worked hard, too, and expected the same of Jo Ann.

Sis dusted and ironed and helped Mother make breakfast, wash the dishes, sweep the floor, and launder our clothes in the new gas-powered wringer washing machine. They hung the clothes on a clothesline where the desert sun did its job. We carried water from the well, but washing was easier than in the days when Mom scrubbed on a washboard.

Sometimes Jo Ann and I were alone at home. There was plenty to do. Her work was mostly inside. Mine was outside. She could not iron unless Mom was home because she had to heat the flatiron on the stove. She said she was glad she did not have to help me clean out the chicken house because of the dirty manure I shoveled.

I fed the dogs, pigs, horses, and cows and helped with the heavy "men's" work, but we both fed the smaller animals because they took a lot of care. I was happy getting toys, most of which Dad made. At the farm, Sis and I walked on large, fruit-juice-can stilts. Dad punched two holes in each set and attached binder twine to make toeholds. Up we would go to be suddenly much taller. Off we walked.

Dad also bought us "Monkey," or Montgomery Ward, tricycles when we were little. I always wanted one of those pedal cars but never had one. They cost too much. I valued our toys, but Sis could always find something to run into.

I pedaled hard to haul a couple of squarish two-gallon cans of water on a little platform with two-inch sides. After several trips on my trike through the weeds to the hog pens, I was sweating. The sun threatened to blister my six-year-old neck just as I heard a rattle and ran, screeching, "Snake! Rattlesnake! Dad, come quick!"

Jo Ann and Gary riding their trikes, San Jon farm

He hunted for the snake in overgrown weeds. Sure enough, he found that reptile and killed it with a hoe. After that, I stayed away from dangerous, thick weeds where I could not see what was hiding unless Dad went ahead of me, and we carried the buckets of water. Sis never wanted that job, and none of us liked rattlesnakes.

Sis adored playing with all the cute pups, colts, calves, piglets, lambs, chicks, and kids. We used to have sweet, soft baby lambs, but they grew into stinky sheep. I remember men coming to shear and hearing the bleats. We sold their wool and never ate them. The problem with sheep was they grazed grass so short there was none left for cows and horses. Sheep could be dangerous. Once the big buck sheep knocked Mom down and almost killed her.

"Run! Run to the house. Run!" she screamed.

Afterwards, we kids did not feel safe out there with those

sheep. That buck was terribly mean. I was glad when Dad got rid of them.

Mom ordered chicks from Montgomery Ward for almost $10 per hundred chicks. Jo Ann and I wanted to hurry to the post office almost as soon as the order went off. We expected little blue and yellow boxes with holes to arrive any day.

Daddy and I collected eggs, and he took them to the grocer in town. Shorty sorted them by size and candled them. I watched him do that once. He took a box with a light inside and put an egg partway through a hole on one side of the box. The light let him see inside the eggshell. He said he could see flaws and tell how fresh the egg was. He would not buy fertilized eggs because they had little chicks growing inside. Sometimes the grocer gave me a soda pop, which made the trip even sweeter. Dad called it "sody-pop."

Our parents were away working when Jo Ann asked if I wanted to have a tea party with her and her dolls. I had heard her play like she was entertaining Eleanor Roosevelt. She wore a long strand of beads and one of Mom's little hats with a short veil. She wobbled in Mom's high heels for church. I did not want to play, but overheard her talking as herself, Mrs. Roosevelt, and other "guests." Jo Ann balanced Mom's cups and saucers carefully and stuck out her little finger like society folk, pouring imaginary liquid, "Will you have some tea, Madam?"

Mrs. Roosevelt was dignified and knew many rich, powerful people. Jo Ann played like a confidant, serving tiny imaginary tea cakes dusted with imaginary powdered sugar and sparkling crystals of something imported from an exotic land. She tipped the teapot.

"And how is the world today, Mrs. Roosevelt? Have you been helping the President?"

"I've just returned from a meeting with the Ambassador to England. He understands why we must win the war and help the poor who have lost so much."

Eventually, the tea party talk got more personal. Jo Ann said, "Mrs. Roosevelt, how can life get so uneven? Why do some people have so much more than others?"

Back and forth they went, getting more personal. I quit listening and got involved with something else until I heard, "Just why do they give Brother everything? What makes him so special? He can't even keep up in school. I do all the work right. Even when Daddy helped him, he didn't get much better. Why can't I go to a place like England? I could meet the Queen."

At first, I was mad at her meanness, then stunned, then only a little wounded. What she said was true. I thought Sis did not understand any better than I what was going on in our lives or the world, and she did not like it that she could not change things. Silly tea party, anyway. How dare she involve Mrs. Eleanor Roosevelt in the first place? At school, we had co-ed lessons but were not allowed to play with girl students. Were they all this silly?

Jo Ann told me about what was happening at San Jon Elementary or gave me her opinions about the world. She was proud of getting gold stars from her teachers and had lots of friends. I guess she wanted me to know.

Things were smoother when we listened to the battery-operated radio. It was a floor model and stood a little less than four feet high beside the pot-bellied coal oil stove. Mom kept a crocheted scarf on top to protect the wood. When Sis and Mom were at home during the day, Sis listened to afternoon soap operas and ironed pillowcases and tablecloths, or we listened to operettas together. I also loved country music stations. The radio stood in the largest of our three rooms, not counting the kitchen, and we listened to *Lux Radio Theater, Amos and Andy, Lum and Abner,* and other shows. At night Mom crocheted, ironed, or read by kerosene. Dad pored over the six-page *Tucumcari Daily News.* It felt strange not to sit up with respect to hear President Franklin Delano Roosevelt speak to us in his *Fireside Chats* because I had heard him all my life, but he stopped them in 1944 when hard economic times got better. It was not long till FDR died. Now we had President Harry S. Truman.

When we were alone, Jo Ann could be sly and wheedling.

"Come on, Brother, share with me. Don't worry. You'll get your money back someday. I only need a little bit, but I need it bad. You can trust me."

Mom gave us an allowance every week. Sis never had enough cash to buy all she wanted. When she spent hers, Sis talked me out of some of mine and did not pay me back. Jo Ann surmised I must not be smart with money because it worked every week. It was not that I did not know I was being tricked, but I gave her some when I was home because she always had a good story about why she needed it. Whatever I wanted I saved for and waited a long time till I could buy it. I never ran out completely until I bought something nice. My bank was shuttered during the school year because I was far away, so I did not know how she managed.

Sometimes she was unkind. I told her a little about my school, but it hurt when she was mad at me because she acted like she thought I was getting a reward by being away from home. Did she think I was off having a good time while she was left to do chores?

Sometimes I was happier being alone. I pretended it was the first morning I was living at school, and I was Dad. I guessed what he did that day and moved among the animals and pretended it was stormy. Regardless of conditions, the beef and dairy cattle had to be fed without fail, so I was valiant and hardy. The dogs, horses, chickens, and pigs ate their share, too.

I acted out Dad's favorite yarn about delivering milk from the homestead to the creamery in Alamosa, only I changed it to suit myself. Sitting on a little stool, I moved my hands up and squeezed downward to strip milk into my imaginary bucket. My fingers felt the teat release the flow, "psst." I drove my truck with the milk twenty miles to Crescent Creamery in Tucumcari, which in my imagination was the big cottonwood tree between the house and the barn, and I thought how Dad told the story.

"I tied two eight-gallon cream cans onto the saddle horn and rode my horse Ball-ee the sixty miles from Tres Piedras, New Mexico, to Alamosa, Colorado," Dad told us. "Those cans shook so much that by the time I got there that milk had turned to butter, but the creamery didn't mind. Guess a horse is a purty good churn."

Sometimes I acted out the whole story, then went into the kitchen for homemade bread slathered with Mom's homemade butter and chokecherry jam.

I was lighthearted and played and did chores without concerns, except I was terrified by rattlesnakes, loud noises, and strangers at the door. I spent time in the house listening to the radio, made my own sandwiches, and entertained myself for hours. One day, the unexpected sound of a loud knock on the front door startled me. Country people showed hospitality and reacted positively if someone came to the door needing help. My parents were that way but taught us kids to be wary. It was unusual for anyone to knock in the middle of the day.

Neighbors and friends would have gotten what they needed out in the barn or from the well house and would have called out, not knocked. I was cautious and opened the door a bit to find two fellows, strangers, who tried to persuade me to unlock the screen door and let them come in for food. I said no, but they insisted. I picked up an old military rifle, which Dad kept by the door. They left, but I was scared and wished some grown up, anyone I knew, would come. I understood it was important to be suspicious of weird-acting adults and older teens.

At school, I got surprised when someone came up to me unexpectedly.

16 THE TRIALS OF DRY LAND FARMING

Farming was hard because we had dry land, which is much different from having irrigation. Dad cultivated, selected seed, and timed the tilling or listing, planting, and weeding to conserve every drop of the sparse rain that fell, typical of arid New Mexico. The San Jon area had little moisture. Our crops included sugar cane and sorghum grains like hegari (commonly called "high-gear"), maize, and calfer corn (milo maize). We thrashed them to retrieve grain to feed horses, cows, chickens, and pigs. Once we had harvested the grain, the combine collected and bound the stalks into bundles, which we left in the field.

Then we came along the same area and stood the bundles up, teepee fashion, where we left them to cure. When they were dry, we hauled them by wagon to a location where we had placed a tractor with a feed grinder. Watching for hidden snakes, we fed the stalks by hand into the grinding machine. Its output was ground silage used for cow feed. We stored the silage in holes in the ground or in silos above ground where the feed fermented and became animal food, or fodder.

We grew haygrazer for cows to forage on before grasses came in the spring. We raised food crops of melons and garden vegetables that Mom canned or served fresh. Our cheeks, necks and arms tanned in the sun on our 360-acre farm. Without enough rain, we experienced blowing sand from dry, hot wind.

As we spit grit out of our mouths, Dad told Mom, "Remember, New Mexico is The Land of Enchantment. All it needs is a drink."

"No, Tood, it's an old sandhill. Not much enchantment on a day like today."

We prayed for moisture. Sporadic, welcome downpours sometimes turned on us and caused flash floods that drowned half-grown crops. The muck caked my shoes and hardened the ground into treacherous ruts. New plantings or weeks of work were washed out. The cost was high because of wasted seed and time. Sometimes it was too late to start over. When that happened, life was squeezed out of us. We needed everything we planted. But when a rainbow stretched across the sky after one of those devastating storms, Mom reminded us that it was God's promise to love us always. So, we tried again.

This year of my first summer home from school was extra dry and I was extra happy to be there. I missed working on projects Dad had built, like a lean-to shed to protect the animals from bad weather and the corrals of crossties discarded by the railroad. On a day in August, Mom, Jo Ann, Dad, and I sang as we drove back from shopping in Tucumcari. It was a glorious day. We topped a little rise. The world came to a standstill.

"Smoke, Tood. Look." Mom said, pointing out the window.

"Good God! The whole place is on fire," Dad cried, hitting the gas.

My heart jumped in panic at his cry, and Jo Ann leaned across me to stick her head out my window. I could smell smoke before we jumped out of the car. My eyes stung. What if our house were in ruins? Were the animals hurt? Men ran around throwing water at the flames. We joined them, grabbed buckets, dunked them in the horse trough, and attacked the inferno. But it was too late. We watched helplessly as flames devoured the outbuildings and turned corrals to ash. Thankfully, the men had freed the animals. That day I learned neighbors could depend on each other.

"Sorry we couldn't do more, Tood," the men said as they slapped Dad's back.

"That's awright. You kep us from losing ever'thin'. I hate seein' the horses scorched, but none of our animals died because you boys let 'em go."

"We found your gate open but didn't see nobody."

"I figure the fire started when someone came acrost our proppitty to get to Monument Rock along old Route 66. They can't resist its ice-cream cone shape. Things like this happen, but I al'us loved this life. I'll get to rebuildin' termorra."

The fire might have come from a spark off a train or a pickup's exhaust or when a careless hobo passing through flicked a cigarette into the brush. We never knew for sure.

The house was safe. We almost forgot why we had been so happy coming home from the Tucumcari shopping trip. It was the day we had victory in Japan, VJ Day. World War II was over. We had danced with people on the streets and shouted the news, so everybody knew. Everyone hugged and kissed and hollered.

"Thank you, God! Our boys are coming home!" and "No more rationing!"

The horns blasted, and church bells pealed as we laughed. Jo Ann and I jumped up and down and ran to tell whoever we saw.

Mom clapped her hands, "My brothers will be coming home."

Dad bought Cokes and ice cream cones to celebrate. That's why we sang in the car till we got to the rise.

The big war had ended, but we had our own battle to fight. It was time for me to go back to school. I thought of all the work Dad had ahead of him and was sorry I would not be there to clean up and rebuild. I knew that next Christmas I would find new corrals and another barn Dad's two hands had built.

17 PROJECTS AND A BREAKTHROUGH

Summer days of fun, work, exciting war news with victory, mud, and fire ended. I tucked my knife and marbles in the back of the nightstand drawer. The train chugged along the rails to Alamogordo in September 1945. I faced another year of dreaded written braille, but I was going to lick that stuff. I looked forward to music. The violin, a couple of sets of new clothes, and a big box of treats traveled with me.

The Woodie driver met me with news that Mrs. Cole was no longer at New Mexico School for the Blind. That took the breath right out of me.

Miss Ruby Brown taught most of my third-grade classes. I fell in love with her and knew I would do better. Even so, days could not go fast enough. Homesickness set in for the second year. In the first two weeks, I was in the hospital for four days and did not eat much of the popcorn from Mother. I finally admitted I was homesick, but then had some fine days.

I treasured each of Mom's letters, kissed them and traced her writing with my finger to learn her script. My good friend Gus had more sight than I did. He saw me tracing Mom's bold handwriting and said it was called cursive, script, or longhand.

Cursive had letters joined together and was invented to make writing by hand faster. Gus offered to teach me to write like that. We started with my name.

As I practiced writing cursive, I thought about Mother's hands and all the nights she sat crocheting by the light of the kerosene lamp. I paused and could almost see her hands twisting the sturdy cotton and the crochet hooks flying to create a strip of circular patterns. Then another and another as the piece grew. She frowned and tugged the cotton strand.

"Why're you pulling out the thread?" I asked when she ripped out.

"I'm a sorry lot, Son. I missed a stitch. It's no good that way. The design won't be right. It doesn't look like much, but once I have it done and lay it on the bed, that little spot will jump out at me, and I'll never see all the good parts. Got to take it out and start again from there."

She was making a bedspread for a double bed. Someday it would be mine.

"Doesn't it make you mad?" I asked.

"Has to be done, Son. No choice about it. I was over to Emily's place and could see right off where she kept going when she should have ripped out. In crochet, every mistake shows. Hers looked crooked and the edges did not line up. My mother taught me to rip and redo, and she was right to be particular."

That was my mom—always practical—no waste—creating beautiful patterns that would last for years without unraveling, secured by sturdy knots. Like my heart, held together by knots of hope and loss and dreams.

My life was like the sisal lasso and braided quirt handle Dad knotted or Jo Ann's hair twisted tight in braids not to be undone any time soon. It was wound tight by heartache—by lonely train rides, an upset tummy, or dots that eluded the touch of my fingers. Like my mother's quilts, my life was made of sturdy fiber woven into a beautiful pattern. Never to unravel. No sirree. Not in this Western. My heroes were tough, and so was I. They did their best to get along and make things better. That's what I would do.

I placed Mom's letter in the drawer of my nightstand. From that day, I got along with people the best I could, and every morning I woke up ready to go.

Of course, even when I learned to write cursive, I would be required to use braille. Miss Brown began teaching me braille signs, which are shortcuts for certain words, but said I was not yet ready to write my letters home, so I dictated.

"Dear Mom, we have chorus every Monday and Wednesday. The hymns we are learning in chapel are beautiful. Soon I might play them on the violin. I like all my teachers and my big geography book and have a lot of other books. I finished the brush I was making in shop and started another one. There are about twenty boys in swim class but only six or eight when we learn new games in gym.

"Our third-grade class has lots of good times, like going to the picture show. Abbott and Costello talked about baseball, and we laughed so hard that Tony fell out of his seat. We tried to say *Who's on First?* all the way home. You must see *Naughty Nineties.* I want to see it again. Maybe we can go when I come home."

I asked Miss Brown to end with, "Tell Jo Ann that I said hello. I would like to see her. I would like to see you and Daddy, too."

Too bad Jo Ann could not take shop because she would like to make her own little brush, and she would like my teacher, Mr. Thomkins. Classes were small. Projects were useful, and the teacher told us exactly what to do.

"You are going to make a scrub brush—the kind used for scrubbing fingernails. You'll need the vise standing next to you," my shop teacher said. "I'll come around to all six of you, one at a time, and show you how. First, examine your two pieces of wood and tell me what you learn about them."

I picked up the two pieces of wood in my workspace and ran my fingers along them. The thicker piece had rows of predrilled holes. The thinner one was smooth.

Macario said, "They are not alike. One's thinner."

"You're right," the teacher said. "Lay the thinner piece aside. It's only one-eighth inch thick, and you'll use it to finish your brush. Now, run your fingers over the top and bottom surfaces of the thicker piece. It's one-half inch thick. What do you feel?"

"Holes," I said. "Holes on both sides, but there's something wrong with mine."

"What's wrong?"

I held the straight wooden piece up where he could see it. "The holes on top aren't as big as the ones on the bottom."

"You're doing a good job examining the wood. Don't worry. There's nothing wrong with yours," Mr. Thomkins told me, then went on. "Class, the holes on the top are only one-sixteenth inch in diameter, but the bottom holes are one-fourth inch. Feel them carefully. Can you tell the top from the bottom? You need to know the difference when you put the bottom into your vise."

Dad taught me to pay attention to different sizes when we drilled. Even though they were big enough for me to see, the teacher had me feel the holes. When I looked through from the bottom, I could tell they lined up but only went partway because I saw a tiny opening of light.

"Put your wood into the vise with the top on the side closer to you."

I passed a very thin copper wire through the tiny opening. If the wire broke, I had to splice it to continue. It was hard to tie on another wire. We were careful, but every one of us broke a wire and sometimes pricked our fingers.

We'd hear, "Ouch!"

"Oh, no."

"Shoot, I've gotta do it again."

None of us liked to have to splice that wire and got upset when that happened, but we still had to do it.

To construct the brush, I made a loop with the inserted wire and then filled that loop with a group of stiff yellow fiber bristles called a tuft. I pulled the wire taut, and the tuft folded in half. I repeated this process going left to right, left to right, until all six or more rows of holes were filled. I was stitching with the wire. Then I used small brads through two small holes to attach the thinner piece of wood so that it covered the wires and made a top for the brush.

"This looks good," the instructor told me.

I was proud.

"Let me shear the tufts to give them an even edge," he said.

I was proud my brush was finished, but I was not done before the boys with no sight. Just as with reading braille, I watched them turn out the work much faster than most of us with sight. Their blindness let them rely on touch and not be distracted by other cues around them. This was a simple brush, but I needed agile fingers. I had to understand the whole process to size the tufts to fit in the holes. Then I had to pull the wire to secure one tuft before going to the next hole.

Brush making was appealing so I didn't mind making a few more of different sizes and purposes. Mr. Thomkins said I would make a broom the next year. The brushes were interesting for a while, but I wondered how soon we would move on to something else.

The biggest news was the letter I brailled all by myself on September 28, 1945:

I got your package and letters. I am making brushes and brooms tomorrow. I am going to gym today. We are going to have swimming tomorrow, and I want to learn to swim better. Your loving son, Gary

My success did not last. Miss Brown told me she would write for me in October because my letter was not good enough. I had a lot to say at Halloween, so I was glad not to have to punch all those codes again when I told about my clown costume with its funny hat with coarse, red-yarn hair sticking out. Or how I got to stay at our Halloween party enjoying good refreshments until about ten. Then I told about other things.

"I got a lot of mail. Thank you for my suit, which fit fine. Don't worry about it because my new housemother, Mrs. McDonald, said she will take care of it for me. I like all my teachers, even the new one in gym. I am swimming better than ever.

"The thing I am proudest of is learning a new violin piece. I can play nearly all of it. I have two lessons a week and practice three days a week. Please bring my guitar when you come to see me."

"Be sure to ask when they are coming," I told Miss Brown.

"Anything else, Gary?"

"Mom, I like school better this year. I am reading better and know all my braille signs. I can write good when I take my time and think.

"Tell Jo Ann hello. I would like to see her. I will be glad when Christmas comes and will write to her next time. Answer soon."

On November 15, I wrote my next letter in braille.

I am in school. I like my teachers fine.

Can Uncle Wheeler come to see me?

We went to the White Sands the tenth. We had a good lunch.

We are going to have a skating party.

Please send me some money.

18 ARITHMETIC AND BASKETS

Arithmetic and I were getting along well after Miss Brown gave me a thin, seven by twelve-inch arithmetic slate. I was excited to learn to use it. It had a rectangular frame of stainless steel with over 400 eight-sided holes punched into it, little octagons. I did not count them, but I did count the lead type. There were thirty-eight identical pieces of lead type that were about one-half inch long. That was why it was called a Type Slate. Each piece had a raised bar on one end and two points sticking out the other to tell me whether I was working with numbers 1-8 or 9 and 10. Each piece of type had four sides. I learned to represent 1 through 10 and what to do with them by the way I stood the type in the holes and whether the bars or the points were on top. It was another code.

We started with addition and subtraction. There was a tray at one side where I stored unused type. After a while, Miss Brown showed me how to multiply and divide, even to do long division.

The type was heavy, which made it easy to handle but also to drop and lose. I had a little bag to store my type in, but had to use my allowance from home to buy more anytime some got lost. That was why I counted them. I could set up and solve problems on my slate in the same way sighted people do with pencil and paper. As the problems got harder, the code became tedious enough to encourage lots of us to excel at mental math because we could take mental math with us anywhere we went, like home.

Christmas of the second year approached. I had to concentrate to finish the basket I wanted to take. Dad caned chairs for our dining table. I had an idea basketmaking was kind of like caning. As I wrote my Christmas letter, I thought Mother would like a new basket to put something special in.

Dec. 12, 1945. Braille letter.

Dear Mother and All,
I am in school.
I want Santa Claus to bring me a bicycle.
I am glad that I am going home for Christmas.
We are going to sing some songs. They are "Come Blow
with a Noise" and some other songs.
I am weaving a basket in shop.

In the next class, Mr. Thomkins told us, "Find the round or oval piece of plywood on your desk. It has holes equally spaced around the edge. What do you think the holes are for?"

"Are we going to weave in and out of these all the way around?"

"Almost, but not quite. Find the stiffened straws and hold one so it stands like a soldier, straight and upright."

He waited till everyone had time to do it, then said, "Your straw is called a stave."

Following directions, I bent each stave to let me weave it into one hole and back up through the next before choosing another and weaving it through two more holes. I tried to get all of them as even as possible at the top, but they were a little ragged. Mr. Thomkins helped me even them with shears. Then I helped some boys with no sight cut theirs.

"Gary, your staves are done. Now you are going to weave the straws wrapped with colored cellophane in and out of the staves, in and out, in and out, all around until the side of the basket rises as high as you want it to. Let me get you started."

I squinted to see what he was doing and was ready to try it myself. It was not as simple as it looked, but the bowl of my basket started rising. At the top, I had to leave enough material to plait what was above the woven part, about two fingers' worth. When I got that far, I asked, "What's next?"

Mr. Thomkins started plaiting my leftover staves to make a nice braided edging. It was my first experience doing that, but I'd seen Mom braid Jo Ann's hair, and Dad was always good at plaiting string or rope. The teacher let me finish it, and I noticed the totally blind students were quicker than I was with our first baskets. I made a few more on other days, and it was still true. I did not mind being slower but would be happier when Mr.

Thomkins moved us on to something else. He was a good teacher and always gave us time to finish old pieces if we got behind.

Baskets were useful and popular, but I decided I hated making them.

Braille letter from Gary, December 1945

19 MY BEGINNINGS

Jesus saw a man blind from birth. His disciples asked him, "Rabbi, who sinned, this man or his parents, that he was born blind?"

"Neither this man nor his parents sinned," said Jesus, "but this happened so that the work of God might be displayed in his life."

Jesus opened the man's eyes, and he could see.

John 9:1-3 NIV, Holy Bible

Inside the rawhide suitcase were a brush and braille magazines. I carried a basket to fill with goodies at home during Christmas of 1945.

We strung popcorn and cranberry chains and draped them on the tree. Little crocheted stars, silver balls, and poinsettias made of satin ribbon hung suspended from green branches. When we lit the candles, it was perfect magic. Cinnamon, pumpkin, turkey, and chocolate smelled delectable. Mom tied a red bow on my basket and filled it with bonbons. We sang along with music from the radio. Some of my relatives came for a big dinner and talked and laughed. That included Mother's brothers, home from the war.

We joked around because our family was lucky, but times were serious. Not everyone made it back, and some of those who returned had bad memories. Dad said they were shell-shocked. I stayed near the men to hear a little about my uncles' experiences. Uncle Doc was at sea with the Coast Guard. The army sent Uncle Luther to the Ascension Islands. Uncle Wheeler was in Guam and the Far East. Wheeler received the Philippines Liberation medal. He said he flew very low over Tokyo the day of the Japanese surrender, low enough he could see people's faces. He was probably in a B-29.

My youngest uncle was Liston. He loved the B-29. He enlisted at seventeen. My grandparents gave special permission for him to go. He was training to be an Air Force pilot but worried because he got airsick. He served in England and Germany with a fellow named Clark Gable and was my hero.

Dad had a larger family. Most of them lived on ranches near Portales, New Mexico. We saw them several times during the year, but they celebrated Christmas in their own homes. They were probably happy like us because Dad's brothers, Clyde and Fred, came back safe, too. I would see all of them for Granny Montague's birthday in July.

I counted all my uncles who went to war. A couple of days after Christmas I asked, "Why didn't you go to war, Dad?"

"I checked in with the Draft Board every month. They said I was 'scused. They said our farm and dairy businesses were too important to the community to let me leave."

*Uncle Wheeler Moore
in WWII uniform
holds twins. Gary squints.
Windmill in background.*

*Uncle Liston Moore
wears aviator's helmet,
goggles, and flight jacket*

*Uncle Luther Moore
waves in front of troop train*

"Boy, I never was one not to take up my part and do it good. But I couldn't help what they decided about leaving me home. I done took care of my family and folks hereabouts."

I was glad the army refused to take him. Who would have looked after Mom and Sis once I left home?

He was in a talkative mood but was matter-of-fact about how hard life had been leading up to when I was born.

"The Depression was hard on us and the whole nation. We struggled to save enough cash to buy kerosene and coal for heatin' and cookin'. It was tough to get basic buildin' materials like lumber, nails, and paint, so we got 'em a little at a time. It warn't no diff'runt fer nobody else. We all had troubles. Just as it done started to git better, the war began. That made supplies short because a lot of what we needed was used by the army and rationed for the rest of us."

"Like what?" I asked.

"Your Mom and I had coupons in a ration book. If we had enough, we bought what we needed."

"I remember when she used them at Shorty's for groceries and saw you do it when you went for gasoline and kerosene," I said.

"Yessir. They were for flour, sugar, chocolate, bananas, even her crochet thread. I might have to wait for chicken wire and farm equipment. Everything was scarce. Gasoline I bought for farming cost less and had blue colorin' to identify it as such, almost like the bluin' Mom puts in wash water to whiten our clothes. People caught usin' tractor fuel in other vehicles or fer other things were severely fined. We're still tryin' to git prosp'rous agin."

"That wasn't fair to farmers."

"Look here, Boy. That was necessary. When Ol' Man Have-To gets after you, you do it."

As we worked around the farm, he pointed out equipment and how he dealt with rationing. He bought farm machinery and implements from Montgomery Ward and Sears, Roebuck and Company, unless he could find used equipment for less at farm auctions. Poultry raisers and farmers who could afford to purchase new equipment were required to have a Rationing Certificate from the local rationing committee. That meant he signed a statement saying items were for production and care of crops, livestock, or produce on a farm. Even horse-drawn planters required the statement. There were many things he needed:

Planting, seeding, and fertilizing machinery;

Plows, such as listers, harrows, knife sleds, and cultivators;

Harvesting combines, tractors and engines;

Farm wagons, cream separators, milk cans and lids; and

Hand pumps for airing tires on wagons and trucks.

"Life was hard, but we never went hungry."

A few days later, I rode on the Rock Island and Southern Pacific headed to Alamogordo and enjoyed baked-from-scratch cookies. I let the crumbs tickle my tongue and linger longer than necessary before swallowing.

I had begged Mom to let me stay home, but she told me, "You must go, Son. You remember how inspiring Winston Churchill was during the war. You liked him. He said doing our best is not enough. We must do what is necessary. That was how we won the war, and that is how you will succeed."

I thought about stories Mom and Dad had told me. Our family did not have much in the olden days, and everything was hard back then. My Christmas 1945 visit seemed short but was not rushed like the previous year's, and Mom and I had lots of time to talk because we did not travel. She told me she was proud of me, said I had grown a lot and that she was surprised I knew so many new words. Everybody was happy to see me, and I had a great time. In a serious moment, Mom said she had ideas about what might have damaged my eyes. I really did not remember much about what she said on the train so long ago.

"I want you to know what happened when you and Jo Ann were born. We don't know exactly why your eyes are bad, but sometimes things happen when babies are born."

Wince. I thought no, maybe I didn't want to hear.

Then, yes, I did want to know. She talked about the forceps, oxygen, my small size, moving back to the Tres Piedras homestead with its fierce winters, falling, my near death from pneumonia, and how all those things could be the cause. She said God gives us strength to handle the crosses we bear, and sometimes what happens to us is nobody's fault.

I liked the parts about Ball-ee in the snowstorm and the whiskey and was glad the army said Dad's work at home was helping the war effort. Somehow, I felt more grown up because they had explained so much.

Long train rides were good for thinking.

Golden State Passenger Train on its way to NMSB,
courtesy of Southern Pacific Historical and Technical Society
circa 1940s

20   A LASTING VICTORY

Jan. 14, 1946.

Report to Parents from Ruby Brown.
   The work which Gary does with his hands is usually poor,
   but his mental work is excellent. He is improving in reading
   and spelling. His letter in braille is not well written this
   time. Gary is doing especially well in history and nature
   study. He forgot to mention that he received his package.
   He is always pleased with his mail.

It had been almost a year and a half when there was a breakthrough
that lasted. I wrote two letters in braille.

Jan. 29, 1946. Braille letter.

Dear Mother and Father,
   We had a distinguished speaker.
   We had a dance Saturday night.

We had things to eat and then danced.
How is my dog Tip? I hope he is fine.

I only called Dad "Father" because Miss Brown said that was the right way. I liked "Mother" but "Father" was not what we said. Miss Brown had someone write the solution of the braille code on the letter, so my family could read it. There was room to write small script above each line of code. When we put my letter into the envelope, I could not stop smiling. I felt tender and strong at the same time, warm and relieved. My fingers danced through the air with pleasure. They had done what my brain told them and deserved to be excited. Two weeks later, I had another success.

Feb. 15, 1946. Braille letter.

Dear Mother and Father,
   A speaker came last Monday. He was very good.
   He talked about Turkey.
   I have almost learned my violin piece. It is getting better. It is getting easier too.
   Please send me my paper punch and tell me the name of our neighbors.
   I want to come home with you.
   I will work and work.
   Your loving son, Gary

P.S. from Miss Brown - Do you notice any improvement?
Hope so, as his writing is much better.

Little connections to home meant a lot to me, like my dump truck, guitar, and office tools for making perfectly formed holes. Would any of them get to me?

Miss Brown told me about Helen Keller. She could not see or hear but learned to speak and talked with the President. I heard her voice on the radio once. It sounded a little odd, but I understood her words. Miss Brown said Helen Keller believed the most beautiful things in the world were not seen with eyes or touched with fingers. Beautiful things were seen with the heart. My heart was full.

We listened to poetry in class. Most of it rhymed. Sometimes we clapped a beat or added our own lines. Miss Brown recited poems about beauty and kindness, about the majesty of the mountains and the glory of the seas, and about living every day with hope and love.

On Sundays, we took a school bus to the church our parents chose. Every student was required to attend church. Miss Brown also led me in Protestant Bible study on Thursday nights while Catholics were at confession. She said it was important to take care of our spirits as well as our bodies and minds. She had almost no sight and showed us we could learn by listening and remembering. She said her job was to do what our parents would do if we were at home, that it was our job to learn all we could and make them proud of us. She made me feel clean and light with no worries, even when she demanded more.

In chorus, we sang the state song "O Fair New Mexico" and our school song until we were perfect. They had the same tune. We would sing them for Elizabeth Garrett, the composer of both, who was an operatic soprano who became nationally known as the Songbird of the Southwest. She was blind. She taught at NMSB in the early 1900s. I knew about Billy the Kid and Sheriff Pat Garrett, who shot him. I was surprised to learn the sheriff was her father. Her visit was a big occasion. She shook my hand and said she liked our singing. She told us we would all be successful and self-reliant, and we should be unafraid to try the impossible.

Elizabeth Garrett met Helen Keller when they worked for the American Red Cross. She brought Helen to New Mexico in 1925 to persuade our Legislature to provide money for our school. Mr. Ditzler, the chorus teacher, told us that was important in the history of NMSB. That was when our school's name was changed from the Institute for the Blind to the New Mexico School for the Blind. He said Helen had been honored as a New Mexico treasure.

21 IN THE CULTURE OF THE BLIND

Our coach was also Scout Master of the troop for boys on campus. I had longed to be a Scout and joined Cubs. I worked and played hard and respected Scout principles and activities. I was proud of my uniform.

Our school was a tight community where most knew each other. Our activities included other NMSB students, boys with boys and girls with girls. The time schedule and regimen discouraged mixing with outsiders. Except for special events or when we went to church, we usually saw our own people. At our concerts, we were on stage or in the audience. The townspeople who came sat and clapped. Most of the time, there was no mingling with them before or after performances, not even for punch and cookies. Boys my age had to be in bed by seven most nights, so it was a late night for me when I went to a concert or sang.

Ten to twelve girls and boys shared most of my classes, but we were seated separately for other activities. That included chapel services each morning. I still thought girls were not worth much, so separation was fine with me. I had three classes in the morning, with one recess, and three more in the afternoon, with another recess. Sometimes I got lost in thought or a tough project, but there were days I could not wait for bells to signal changes.

We had a routine. That meant we had to do things in a certain way at a certain time. It brought order, a foundation I could depend upon. We had rules about when we went to town for a haircut and how we dressed at school or away from it. Girls wore dresses or skirts and peasant blouses. Now that I was nine I could wear regular street clothes for playing outside. I used to have to wear overalls. For my classes, I wore dress pants, a white shirt with a tie—the cloth kind I had to tie myself—and shoes I shined till they gleamed. I wore a suit on Sunday and for church and concerts. It was what you might call formal at school.

At home, I had worn my suit to church on Sunday, but other days all of us cowboys wore work jeans, western shirts, cowboy hats, and pointed boots. Dad was thin with long arms. Mom starched and ironed his cotton western shirts with two pocket flaps and snapping studs. I dressed like him. No buttons to fumble with and make me late. That's how we dressed every day, except that in cold weather we wore dark coveralls.

Around me at school, I was used to the sounds and sights of boys who saw nothing. I heard shuffling, accompanied by slow, jerky movements, with occasional boyish outbursts when they bumped into walls or doors. I had been a little scared at first. I was shy, and everything seemed strange. I missed my animals and my family and wondered what I could count on and what might change without warning. I could almost taste work with Dad and his tools.

I did not invite trouble. It did not make sense to act up. It was easier to stick to the rules, but last year a couple of us tried to trick a housemother who seemed more interested in entertaining her company than being with us. We heard a story that she had had several husbands and was now a single young woman. While she entertained her soldier boyfriend in her room, we took a rubber band and tied it to a tennis ball, then tied it to the knob of her door. We thought the ball on our side would hit her when she pulled her door inward. We did not stick around to find out. Nobody accused us. We were not punished. She was not here this year, and we wondered if she knew it was us and where she went.

22 THE SUMMER I WAS TEN

I was getting big enough to be a lot of help on the farm and when I went to visit my relatives. It was another blissful summertime except for my tenth birthday. Mom, Sis, and I planned a birthday party. Kids played and chased one another, but I felt ignored. I had been gone for two school years. Didn't they want to play with a blind bat?

Mother scolded me for thinking that way, said I should not feel bad when they had not gotten to know me as I grew up.

"You are not a blind bat, Son. You are a fine young man who can rise above this. They didn't mean anything by it. They were just being kids."

The rest of the summer was more interesting, especially when Uncle Gid, called "The Mule Man" because he was so strong, invited me to stay a few days on his farm. As a younger man, he was a scrapper who would take on anyone, pick a fellow up and throw him in a water tank. He laughed at most anything. One time he fell hard into a wall in his house and put a hole in it. He laughed and said he felt so foolish to be inside the wall. He also was a practical joker. He used electric fencing to keep in his ornery Brahma bull. I asked how it worked.

He said, "Gary Ted, if you touch it, you'll get a great big shock. Now here's the trick, Ted. You stand where it's a bit wet or on a piece of tin and touch the wire, and it won't shock you at all."

Being a naïve kid, I stood in a muddy area and got some sharp jolts. He chortled about tricking me. I applied my new knowledge back home to teach an annoying neighbor a lesson.

He was a windy fellow who always came at the wrong time and was in the way while we were trying to finish milking. Believing my experience made me able to stand more current than most, I laid my hand upon the magneto of our milking machine, powered by a gas generator, and at the same time, I bumped the leg of our neighbor. I wanted to be done soon so we could eat and go to the movie.

After I shocked him, that gentleman took off and never came back at milking time.

Our pigs had an electrified hog pen with a battery-operated charger. One day Dad's back was to me, blocking my way to slop the swine. He was jawing with another neighbor. I could not interrupt them because Dad believed kids should be seen, not heard. I touched the fence and the back of Dad's leg. He moved so fast, he almost ran over our visitor.

Dad's belt made me pay for it on my end.

He should not have been surprised at my jokes because both his brothers, Gid and Fred, pulled tricks. They pulled them on me and everybody else. Uncle Fred was tenderhearted but returned from WWII a bit toughened, Dad said. He fixed anything that broke. He had a houseful of kids and I should come to Portales for a couple of nights, he said. I wanted to go and knew he would move my water glass while I was pouring or tell me his kids could outdo anything I could do. There was lots of laughter, so a short visit was exactly what I wanted.

In July, Mom placed her big roasting pan and a cake carrier in the car. We drove to Portales for Granny Montague's birthday. Besides Gid and Fred and Dad's other brothers, Ed and Clyde, Granny had a houseful because Dad had sisters, too: Gertie, Opal, Mozelle, Mayrene, and Peggy. They did not play tricks like the men did. They made quilts and sewed, cooked, and spent a lot of time bringing up my cousins. Sis and I saw everyone each year when all the families went to Granny's party. There were lots of pots with corn and potatoes, beef and chicken, and several cakes with preserves and apple pies. We helped ourselves and found a place to sit. Granny loved her sons and daughters and was quite religious. She enjoyed cooking and fixing for people who were joyous and having a good time around her. Her children could do no wrong. I believe she said good things about everybody.

Dad told me another sister, Monta, died at seventeen from an appendectomy. He said doctoring was not so good back then.

Granny's boys cherished their mother and adored vehicles. The older ones sat around talking about carefree years when Dad and Ed ran a "motersickle" shop in Plainview, Texas. They enjoyed their ten-hour workdays. They formed a bike club with a dozen riders. I enjoyed all Dad's stories about being with his brothers, such as how Ed took care of a panhandler who pestered Dad.

"I came out of a restaurant and was approached by a panhandler who did not want to move along. Ed took the guy by the arm and told him, 'You go to the other side of the street. This is my side.' The fellow left without question 'cuz Ed was a big man."

In one of his favorites about vehicles, Dad told me about a fancy Ford roadster he owned before marrying. "It'd jis go to cadillacking off until that ol' boy hit it right in the side and bent the frame, so I traded it in fer a motersickle. But a motersickle warn't good for life as a married man, so it went bye 'n' bye, too." He always gave a chuckle with this story. Sometimes he enhanced it with details about balloon tires or the color and finish. Dad sure loved vehicles.

A dozen motorcycles side by side with riders in white shirts,
Motorcycle Club, Portales, New Mexico, 1920's

He also loved horses. He told and retold about when he and brother Fred rounded up wild ponies, called mustangs, over the ninety miles of northern New Mexico between Taos and Tres Piedras. He said the land was full of wild horses. They broke them to ride or sell.

Fred interrupted to remind him of the time they drank too many beers. "We drove the plow horse team fast round and round the Taos plaza, not much knowing we weren't really going anywhere." And then we all guffawed.

Sis and I spent one or two weeks separately with grandparents or aunts and uncles. When I went to Aunt Florence's house, Uncle Red's chuckle and mobile face made me laugh right out loud. He was a city man in Amarillo, Texas, and had red hair. In his gravelly voice, he told stories about when we all lived on the homestead and how cold winters were. I did not remember much about living in Tres Piedras but sometimes thought I did because I remembered leaving the homestead.

He reminded me, "Snow fell continuously for twenty-three days and nights. Alamosa got fifteen inches. We must have had at least that much. We bundled ourselves into the blue '29 Chevy and followed the last snowplow out. You were two or three."

"What about the animals?"

"Your dad and his brothers rode their horses back up there and drove all the livestock to our new place."

"How did they cook on the trip?"

"They took along a chuck wagon just like you see in the movies."

Yep, real cowboys. Uncle Red and the Montague boys. He was a hobo, too.

"I grew up an orphan, you know. I rode the rails as a hobo for a while. Lots of young men did that during the Depression. We had to find a way to survive. I sure enough had adventures."

From what Dad told me, I knew my uncle might be keeping his hardest times private. He liked to laugh and make hard times sound funny and people extra interesting. I loved his stories, but I also loved the little Safeway store near his home because it sold miniature Hershey bars, Mr. Goodbar, and the one with almonds. He also taught me about refrigeration and air conditioning because that was his business. Yes, he was a good storyteller, but he told one that was hard to believe. Uncle Red said the bomb that won the war was tested about seventy-five miles from my school, right there in the desert at a secret place called Trinity.

This was a great summer with lots of visiting. I also played my new guitar and had time for Mom to tell me about her grandfather. I never knew Great Granddaddy Moore, a Baptist preacher who lived to 101 years old. Grandmother Rosa and Granddaddy William Moore, Mother's parents, and their youngest child, Aunt Wanda, lived together in Happy, Texas. Grandmother and Aunt Wanda liked to talk with me and for me to stay with them. They thought what I learned at school was important. I felt that way when I went to Uncle Luther's and Uncle Clyde's, too.

Mom's father, however, was still bedridden. I annoyed him by knocking his radio off the station.

"What did you do? Leave that alone," he yelled at me.

I acted innocent but did it on purpose because Mom told me he was not nice to his family when she was growing up. She said most of his kids left home as soon as they could get away from him. Mom and I had a long talk before this year's visit. She grew up on a farm near Plainview, Texas, where she took care of her five younger brothers and sisters, a big job. Beyond that, her daddy made her go into the fields and pick cotton. She resented how hard that was on her body. He was overbearing, but there was no talking back to him. She had to get down on her knees to pick and fill big sacks, then drag them to a wagon. There was so much bending and lifting that she vowed her kids would never have to work that hard.

She rubbed her back when she told me, "The sun's heat was blistering, and my back ached and ached."

Maybe I could get even with him. Mom said I needed to pray for him, but it was hard.

23 BOOKS TALK

Back at school, David and Joe pushed me in the junior dorm basement, and I retaliated with all the feigned force I could muster. We were tricky as we reenacted Trojan Wars, and my foes would not get away with treachery. We learned about overcoming foibles and clever deceptions through battle games. Our imaginations thrilled to adventures of Captain Blood. We, like Sherlock, sought out clues to solve stories of crime and mayhem. We acted them out and pretended to be heroes and men of strength, ability, and courage.

The outstanding books we read sparked ideas that became our own. I checked out recorded books from my classroom and listened to them in our study area on the first floor of the dorm building, right below our bedrooms. We had many records with stories and others with long books. I chose mysteries, adventures, and westerns.

"You're welcome to check out extras, Gary," the teacher said.

"How do they make these?" I asked her. I was fascinated by the dark, twelve-inch records.

"The company that made the records put an inscribing needle on a wax disk that was smooth and flat and round. Sound was recorded then copied to thick, heavy shellac material which lasts longer than wax. They call it "pressing."

I raised the lid of the blue, wooden Talking Book machine, full of anticipation.

"Run your finger across the record, Gary."

I felt a lot of lines going around. They were very fine, but I could slip my fingernail in just slightly to feel that they had depth. I strained to see what I felt.

She put her finger near mine.

"These close lines are grooves that let the phonograph needle run in them as the record revolves. Sound comes through a speaker. The twelve-inch diameter talking book record turns at half the speed of a regular record you can buy in a store. The more grooves there are, the longer the record plays before needing to be turned over, up to fifteen minutes on each side. On shorter recordings there are fewer grooves."

"Where do you get these?"

"Our phonographs are loaned to us by the government."

Using the Talking Book amazed me, especially when I learned Uncle Sam was involved in providing these things for kids, the same Uncle Sam who hired the soldiers I saw on my first train ride. There was electricity at San Jon Elementary, but we had no talking books. No braille either. I could not take a phonograph home to share with Sis because there was no way to play it without electricity there.

I loved my days with Talking Book records.

Dormitory, New Mexico Institute for the Blind, circa 1906,
photo courtesy of New Mexico School for the Blind and Visually
Impaired, the Tularosa Basin Historical Society Museum,
and HAI

24 DAILY LIFE

"Gary, the whistle's blowing. Wake up." It was roommate Gus. I had heard the 6:00 a.m. sawmill whistle but didn't want to let him know I was awake.

It blew again. "Beat ya to the line. I'll be first today."

Up I came and hurried to the bathroom to shower and brush my teeth. Back to the bedroom to dress as fast as I could. Fingers fought buttons, then shoelaces. I finished. With sheets turned down to air the bed while I was at breakfast, I raced down the stairs and out to join the line in front of the dorm, ready to walk with the guys to the dining hall. Sure enough, my alarmist was up ahead, but I did not care. It was not half past seven yet. I was on time and could chat with my dormmates.

In the dining room, I sat in my assigned place at the table waiting politely for breakfast. A maid brought a cart with serving platters and placed the food on our table. A student with some sight served our plates and passed them to us. Today was my turn to serve. I did it often. We were polite, but sometimes had heated debates because this was a fine time to visit while we enjoyed a good breakfast of pancakes with bacon and eggs or juice with milk and cereal. The maid removed empty plates, and a houseparent dismissed us when all at our table finished eating. We made sure to be done in time to return to our rooms to make our beds. I knew if I did not get mine made by the time a supervisor checked during the day, I would lose playtime or be required to sit in my room for punishment. None of us wanted that.

I prayed, "Lord, help me to get my bed ready so I can play with the other kids and not get punished. Thank you for hearing my prayer. Amen."

With my bed made, corners tucked in neatly and sheets pulled taut, I was in line for chapel by half past eight Monday through Friday. The chapel service in the auditorium was always a beautiful time. It was interdenominational, Christian, and mandatory. We heard a Bible reading, sang hymns, listened to an interlude, and prayed. Since I had to be in class by 9:00, chapel was a nice way to begin my day.

Lunch was at noon, dinner at 5:30. They proceeded the same way as breakfast, with lining up, a server, and dismissal. For both lunch and dinner, we had one entrée, vegetables and fruit: beef stew, roast beef with mashed potatoes and gravy, grilled cheese sandwich with coleslaw, bologna sandwiches and potato salad, or fried chicken with corn. We always had fish on Fridays. When we had hamburgers for dinner, some of us ate five or six. The bakery smells emanated from kitchen ovens every day. I always inhaled deeply. We had fresh bread, rolls, or biscuits that were mouthwatering and flaky. Daily desserts were fruit cocktail, an apple, tapioca or chocolate pudding, pineapple slices or another fruit or flavor of pudding, but never pie or cake except on special days. We had milk and butter at every meal, but seldom any cheese.

All of us got the same size apples and oranges. One of my teachers said they wanted to treat us the same.

After lunch on weekdays, I was back in class at 1:00. I liked to learn, but the highlight of my day was the whole hour of free time we enjoyed starting at 4:30 p.m.

With hands washed and nails clean, we were in line for dinner at 5:30.

Now that I was older, I had study hall from 6:30 to 7:45, followed by more free time.

"Hey, Gary, let's...." A bud suggested an activity, and we played games or music or whatever we wanted to do inside or outside. We had cards and dominoes with braille dots, which boys with no sight felt as they played. Our checkers fit into holes and had dots for color. I walked the track with a friend many nights. By 9:00, my roommates and I were in our bedroom and by 9:15, in bed.

"Lights out," one of us hollered when the 9:30 bell rang.

The weekends were freer, but we had more chores. On Saturdays, we changed our sheets like we always had. As we got older, all of us also scrubbed tile floors and stairways on hands and knees. We did not mind because we were part of a big family keeping our home nice. The maids, like my friend Eddie's mother, cleaned the bathrooms and other areas.

For some reason, the school's dress code relaxed after I was there a couple of years. We boys stopped wearing neckties, which sometimes had smelled sour from spilled food. No more fussing with ties except on Sundays and special occasions.

I also learned it was best to stick to the schedule and not go wandering around alone during free time. That was a big lesson. One evening, I heard laughter and went onto the playground to check it out. In only a moment, I was accosted by two older boys, much bigger than I was, who grabbed at my clothes, pushed and shoved me till I fell onto the hard dirt. They jumped on top of me.

"No! Stop! Let me go. Leave me alone. Don't!"

They attacked me until I heard their final shout of triumph as they ran off. I regained my senses, got to my feet, staggered a bit, and retreated to my empty room. We were watched so carefully that somebody should have come running to rescue me. How did I end up alone with those two big boys? I remembered their rough hands and how they pushed and tripped me on purpose. They laughed in such a mean way. I could not remember that they said anything. No English. No Spanish. My mind was blank about any words. Did they know me? What made them so fierce?

After I was done with anger and self-pity, I determined to stay away from older boys unless I knew my friends or teachers were nearby. I would not be easy prey.

I would concentrate on going home soon for Christmas, where I would enjoy my family and all of Mom's magic. She made Christmas extraordinary with gorgeous handmade decorations, magnificent tabletop trees and wreaths of burrs, seeds, nuts, and pits she had gathered and glued together. Packages in festive wrappings, decorated with scenes made of papers or felt and tied with colorful cloth bows, would beckon from beneath a glittering tree. She sewed and sequined tablecloths and tree skirts, handcrafted gifts, and cooked morsels flavorful enough to make my mouth water weeks ahead in anticipation. She spared no effort for these joyful celebrations. I looked forward to being at home.

When I arrived at the house a few weeks later, however, I was shocked. There were no decorations.

"Mom, where's the tree? Do we have to go buy one?" Panic rose when I did not see the boxes of decorations we hung from branches every year. "What's going on here?"

"Now Son, I was just too tired this year with all there was to do at home and the store," she began strongly, almost defensively. "I decided not to put up a Christmas tree because," her voice trailed off, "we're going to Grandmother's house in a couple of days."

What a lesson that was to be for both of us. I could not believe the tragedy of not having a tree and learned traditions can never be taken for granted. Mom saw how disappointed I was. She promised we would never go without again.

We had a trickster at the store one night when all of us worked. It was crowded. Someone ran up a big tab for a cowboy hat, several pairs of pants, and shirts. He wrote out a check, and Mom slipped it into the cash drawer without looking at it. In those days, counter checks were not personalized with names. She did not notice he signed the check "U R Stuck." She wondered through the holidays who did it until he came in chuckling and paid up. We had a good laugh.

When I got back to NMSB, we were checked for lice. It was mostly younger kids who needed treatment from Nurse Redding. I never had lice but thought the remedy must be unpleasant and embarrassing. A few needed it when they first came to the school and every time they returned from home, but there was not much trouble with the critters.

My friends and I hiked in the mountains with Cubs. It was fun, but my socks were not comfortable because the housemothers dipped the heels and toes in paraffin to keep them from wearing out quickly. I was lucky that Mom sent me a small wardrobe to last through the year, unless I spurted more than expected. Many kids had only what the clothing bank provided. We grumbled about the socks.

We also had fun reading more adventures by record. Before I knew it, the coldness turned to breezy March. The sand blew. Grains of white blew from the dunes all the way to school. I laughed and played games at spring parties. I sang beautiful pieces in chorus and enjoyed playing my second violin. It was full size to fit my larger hands. Mom loaned the half-size one to a cousin.

Mother sent letters every week. I knew I could count on them and her packages of treats and cash. I was getting tall and needed longer pants.

25 DEATH AND FAITH

I was twelve and now owned my first wristwatch, exactly what I wanted for my birthday. It had a black leather band. I pulled a small stem out to its stopping point and turned it to set the time. The spindly hands on the dial pointed to the minute and the hour, black numbers on a white dial. I set it precisely and would never be late again with the time right there on my left wrist. I would not be late to the train, either, and arrived in Tucumcari on schedule to learn my mother had made an appointment for me to see an eye doctor in Dalhart, Texas.

Five years of long bus rides every three months from the time I was three until eight flashed before my eyes. Attempts to improve my vision had been futile. Nevertheless, we drove ninety-one miles to Dalhart. I thought the man was a quack because he took a speedy look at my eyes, held up fingers, said I was doing fine, and ushered in the next patient. He disappointed us and was expensive. At least, he did not frighten me with talk about surgery to straighten them.

We took another trip in a short caravan of neighbors. Everyone was going to attend a faith healing revival meeting in Amarillo, a hundred miles away. The wind blew fiercely. I knew a well-known evangelistic healer would pray for my eyes to see better. Inside the huge revival tent, I went forward and joined a line of people with afflictions: a man on crutches, a woman moaning on a cot carried by her children, the deaf and mute, some hobbling or crying out in pain, the old, the young, a woman carrying a baby.

When my turn came, the evangelist laid his hands on my eyes and declared, "Heal! Heal!"

There was no difference. I could not see his face any better. "It didn't work. It didn't work, Pastor," I said.

"You don't have enough faith to be healed," he said to me, then turned to the crowd.

"We must have faith that stays strong even in adversity. Pray for strength. Pray for faith that grows so you can be healed."

I went back to my seat angry and hung my head in despair, powerless, and embarrassed. Surely, not many pre-teen boys had as much faith as I did. A shadow of failure and disillusionment hung over me. I became more impatient and fierier every time I thought of it. I felt like the preacher meant I was not a good enough person to see.

The neighbor girl who went with us threw away her glasses and declared, "I am healed." Her vision loss was small, and I was not convinced she was any different than when she entered the tent.

The wind howled after my family came back from the altar. The canvas tent shook. The service kept going. My tension grew.

Finally, the crowd was released and fled in terror. Huge poles supported the tent. Each was about a foot thick. Four big sturdy-looking fellows held onto each one of the poles, trying to stabilize it. Those fellows bounced around trying to keep that tent from collapsing. The steel sign about thirty to forty feet wide and at least a yard high weighed over a ton. It fell but hit no one. It said, "Let Your Faith Loose!"

The revival tent collapsed. Debris hit Jo Ann in the back, frightening all of us. Eighty-five people were hurt but none seriously. I heard that the evangelist did not use tents after that night. I wondered if he ever healed a visually impaired person with eyes like mine.

We drove home but returned to Amarillo the next morning to attend the service. It was held inside a nearby church. I did not want to go, but we all did. I sat there trying to figure out what good had come out of it.

When we got back home, Sis shared her books with me. She put me right there with the March family. Not that Alcott's *Little Women* was one I would have picked for me, but I liked to listen as my sister shared what she loved. It fit our summer because of its sadness. The Marches struggled because their Dad was off in the Civil War. The sweet sister named Beth died, and Jo Ann cried and could not go on for a moment.

When my movie heroes faced death, they became flamboyant, swaggering as without fear. They showed off and looked great until they dropped. The ladies worried over them, cried over them, and longed for their return. And they came back full of life.

I learned that was not the way it was in real life when my favorite uncle died in a plane crash. I was twelve, he was twenty-six. Uncle Liston Moore was a tech sergeant serving in the U.S. Air Corps. Airsickness kept him from fulfilling his dream to be a pilot. His death left an enduring imprint when his B-29 crashed on take-off after being repaired. A telegram came to Shorty, the grocer, who ran to Mom's store to tell her about her youngest brother. We drove to Tulia, Texas, for the burial. My grieving family had no place to stay. Uncle Gid's friend offered the four of us space in his house. Death can bring people together in unexpected ways and get right in your face.

I learned more about death up close that summer. We had lots of dogs on the farm. I preferred boxers because they were dependable, gentle natured, smart, and easy to train, but we also had hounds. We kept so many pups at home that we found ourselves with fourteen hounds. Our favorite was Old Blue because he was loyal and protective. One thing that was not amusing was the unpredictable arrival of a railroad bum. We never knew when one might come, and some were not nice. To the north, Old Tom's place separated our land from Route 66. The highway brought tramps and other strangers. To the south, our land was bisected by the tracks. That brought trouble in the form of railroad bums. Dad, I, and the blue tic hound encountered a hobo who wanted to talk and share Dad's cigarettes.

"You got a light, Mister?"

Dad gave him a Camel. They puffed and traded words. "Did you come a fer piece?"

"All the way from Oklahoma."

"What direction you goin'?"

"I'm heading to California."

They puffed.

"Been awful dry hereabouts. Crops is dryin' up," Dad said.

"Maybe you'll get showers soon."

They puffed in silence till there was no tobacco left. Dad stomped the exhausted butt in the dirt, making sure it was out. The shabby man did the same.

He said, "Now that I've had a cigarette with you, I'll go down and talk with the missus."

Dad let the blue hound go. The canine took after that shabby scalawag as he skedaddled down the tracks till Dad could see him no more.

The cellar where we stored vegetables caved in shortly after Uncle Liston died. Dad lost most of his leather-working tools and his hound down there.

"That poor dog is in a bad way, and we can't help him," he told me. "You fill the hollow with dirt and leave Old Blue in peace."

I did just that, but it hurt. Death hurt me twice.

Death had been distant before, back when Dad shot the hounds that sucked eggs or killed a hen. They were no good on our farm. We needed our chickens and eggs. It was not personal when nineteen sheep were struck on the tracks. The railroad cleaned up the mess. This summer, it cut deep.

When people and animals died, I felt different, but both were great losses and inspired me to higher ideals. I began to think about death and ask what life was about.

26 CAN'T YOU FIX IT?

Another summer and school year flew by. There were big changes. One was Mom's day visit, and the second was one of my new teachers.

Mrs. Celia Quimby, my fifth-grade arithmetic teacher and a hard driver, emphasized mental math. It was important to me that Mom meet her, and she did. I admired Mrs. Quimby for making me believe in myself. I could do anything. I could achieve what I wanted. I could have a good life. Her husband, Neal, was superintendent of our school and the wrestling coach.

Dr. and Mrs. Quimby lived one floor above the library and two floors above the offices in the administration building. It was across the driveway from the auditorium building, which housed a performance area, the kitchen, the teachers' dining room, a bakery, and the maids' quarters. There were also separate dining rooms on opposite sides of the building for girls and boys. I did not know Dr. Quimby well, but I hoped to become one of his wrestlers someday. He had full sight and looked after all the teachers and students. I heard when he wrestled as a young man he missed going to the Olympics by only one two-point decision. That was a tiny margin. He taught me to value fitness and participate in outstanding physical training.

For the moment, I had to be satisfied to think I might someday have the strength of Tarzan and the dash of The Three Musketeers I saw at the movies.

I left braille behind and began reading large print with my eyes. That was my third big change.

I also had a new, challenging question to answer. The eye doctor who examined each student once a year asked me, "Would you like to have your eyes straightened?"

"Will I see better?"

"I'm not saying that. The answer is no, it won't make you see better. In fact, you could have surgery and your eyes still might not be straight. We can't guarantee anything."

"Then my answer is no. Just leave them alone. They don't bother me. I figure if someone else doesn't like how my eyes look, then he's the fellow with the problem."

It had not been long since I went to the faith healer. I knew people poked fun at eyes that looked at each other or danced when they should be still. Children stared and sometimes blurted, "He's got funny eyes." Their parents shushed their children and told them not to cross their eyes because they might get stuck and stay that way.

Comedians aped on stage and audiences laughed because they believed that those of us with strabismus and nystagmus were handicapped and worthy of an asylum. I tolerated their ignorance. Short sightedness can affect the mind not just the eye. They thought people like me looked funny.

At the movies, I enjoyed Mr. Magoo cartoons. He had myopia like I do and got into all sorts of trouble because of his near sightedness. I thought he was funny.

The truth was that strabismus is involuntary and happens when both eyes do not line up in the same direction, so they do not look at the same object at the same time. The iris is not oriented straight ahead of a person. Nystagmus is the involuntary rhythmic movement of the eyes, usually from side to side, that affects the nerves and muscle behind the eyeball and means the eyes dart around so much that maintaining steady focus is difficult. My strabismus and nystagmus distracted some people. I realized it was their own reaction which bothered them, not anything I could fix.

No one contacted Mom or Dad about the doctor's question about surgery to straighten my eyes. Was that a mighty big decision for a twelve-year-old to be asked to make without parental guidance?

A couple of students had cataracts, but that was not my problem. It was possible for a baby to be born with cataracts. Usually it was older adults who developed them, and many of those adults went blind and had glass eyes. I heard a hard-to-believe tale. A doctor removed a lens from a patient's eye, froze it, removed the cataract, and reshaped the frozen lens on a lathe, then put it back in the eye. I heard it worked for a lot of folks.

I put thoughts of surgeries as far from me as possible and concentrated on my studies and movies. Every time I watched a movie with John Wayne I thought about my ranching family. In *Red River*, he headed the first cattle drive from Texas to Kansas along the Chisholm Trail. It was exciting and sad with lots of tough cowboys who had to go west because of how poor people were in the time of the Civil War.

I liked a funny movie called *The Paleface*. It was a story about Calamity Jane and Indians and rifles. I laughed until I almost spilled my popcorn because Bob Hope was so silly.

Pete, who saw nothing, and I listened for hours to talking books and acted out many adventures. I loved *Ivanhoe* by Sir Walter Scott with its major theme of dispossession. At the climax, two of my favorite characters, Ivanhoe and Bois-Guilbert jousted in full armor, stabbing at one another. The drama was electrifying.

Another of my favorites focused on money and power, slavery, the outlaw-king Robin, and society's rules and order. I believed the adventures had been real because I felt the action deep in my body. I knew Robin Hood was right because he took care of the poor.

Shakespeare entered my world. I began to read his plays on talking books, and I never tired of listening to the deep, rich baritone of my favorite narrator.

We also started having a monthly dance in the auditorium on Saturdays. We did the schottische, two-step, and waltz. That's when I met sweet Joycelin. We did not know how to dance, so we sat and talked. I put my arm around her. A few months later, she partnered with another boy at a skating party. Our romance was over. She left NMSB to return to her home and public school.

Meanwhile, I noticed two girls named Liz and Teodora. They looked good and danced well. Where had they been? Liz was in my large-print, sight-saving English classes, but Teddy was with me in math. Teddy had low vision and dressed in stylish clothes, straight wool skirts with matching cashmere sweaters and cardigans. Her pendants were simple but caught my eye. She was the cousin of my roommate, Ventura. We were not allowed to visit or talk much in class, but we began a friendship by sharing candy.

We boys lost our aversion to girls. We learned the dances by watching others or being instructed by our partners. Boys and girls had chairs on opposite sides of the room, so I usually took a girl back to her chair and went to mine after each dance.

Sometimes, we had a campfire. That was where I met Mary Alice and Juanita. School life became more interesting.

27 THE SUMMER I CAUGHT ON FIRE

By the time I was in my teens I decided I hated climbing and camping. I dropped out of Scouts as an Explorer, just about the time Smokey Bear was found at Capitan, New Mexico, not far from school. Smokey climbed a tree during a forest fire and was rescued in May 1950. The United States Forest Service's mascot was already a cartoon bear. Smokey, the real cub, was perfect to warn us to be careful with fire. The radio played a song, which became popular with schoolchildren across the nation. Our mascot was the Golden Bear. The rescued cub was found so close to Alamo that we felt like he belonged to us.

The first thing I did when I went home for the summer was to pedal my bicycle to Shorty's old place with my friend Dwayne.

"Bet I can beat ya down this hill," he said.

"Not a chance." I tried to see how fast I could go. Suddenly my tires slipped on rocks and wham! Pain seared as the handlebars slammed into my ribs. Despite lasting damage, the ride was thrilling.

Even though it was late May, we were surprised by an unseasonal cold snap. Dad and a neighbor were building a laundry and made a fire to stay warm in an area they thought was out of the wind. Several of us kids played nearby when a gust caused sparks to fly from the burning cardboard boxes. Hot cinders fell into the cuffs of my new pants.

"Ouch! Help! I'm on fire," I yelled as the pant leg blew into soft flesh, seriously burning my left leg just above the ankle. There was no doctor in town, but I saw a nurse. I lost chunks of flesh but healed and spent a lot time with Dad at the farm.

The summer dragged as Mom or Dad dressed my leg every day. The cold snap was followed by hot, dry wind. Stony grains bit my face and neck while Dad cut feed and piled it into a big wagon. I was tired of being laid up and staying inside and had begged Dad to let me ride atop the bundles. He gave me a hand up, then jerked the reins. My bottom jostled from side to side, and I was frightened I might fall onto a lurking slitherer. I knew I could not land well or run. That day was nerve wracking, and I was grateful to go back to the house.

Our parents had splurged for a store-bought bedroom set, but their room was too small for the dresser. It sat in the living room. The mirror was poorly made. Wavy lines reflected on the wall beside me when light fell on the glass. Those lines fascinated me. I waved my hands and chased them.

"Brother, you're never going to catch those light beams," Sis teased.

Mom told Dad to take the dresser back and get a better one. I agreed with her. She and I wanted good things, but Dad called it putting on airs. He tended to settle for good enough.

"Nope. I'm not a-gonna do-er," he told her.

He was stubborn and did not want anyone to think he was a showoff, a braggart. Who in the world would have seen Mom's mirror and thought he was a strutting peacock? I remember how thankful he was to buy the icebox that held a fifty-pound block of ice in the top. He did not act like we were putting on airs then, even though we were uptown to have it. He liked a cool drink on a hot day, and Mom had a way to keep food cold. But he would not be swayed about the mirror.

Mother and Daddy gave me the one and only gift I wanted from them—a radio.

"What in the world?" she hollered sternly when she came home to find me sitting on the bed with all the parts spread around. Shocked, she let me know it was expensive and that I had little respect for their sacrifice to give it to me. It had not occurred to me this might happen. I rebuilt the radio. It worked well, and I learned how it was made. She learned I could do it.

That slow summer, I kept from boredom by enjoying cool drinks, playing with light beams, and listening to my radio while I healed. Uncle Clyde came a few times when he could get away from his farm. We sat in the kitchen and had iced tea or coffee. He talked about the sales ring where he bought new calves or reminisced about the summer he lived with us and worked for Daddy. That made me remember Uncle Luther had done the same thing.

Movies offered a few breaks from my boring summer days. Many Sundays our whole family attended, but Saturday had been my day to go alone. I missed most weeks because of my leg but went a few times. I headed there one day, but a talkative fellow kept me out on the sidewalk. He jabbered about the weather or traffic or goings on in the community. The trouble was he was one of the town drunks. I took his shoulders, turned him around, and leaned him against a wall. He kept talking, and I walked into the theater, where I paid twenty-five cents to be admitted and a nickel for a generous bag of popcorn. My favorites were Roy Rogers, Gene Autry, and Red Ryder and Little Beaver. I could stay in my seat for a double or triple feature, all different.

Shorty and his wife, Mabel, brought me a chocolate bar each time they dropped by to play the card game twenty-one or dominoes or Chinese checkers. She cheated to win and laughed when I caught her. Shorty had his hand in many San Jon businesses for years. He was Mom's silent partner in the dry goods store until she could afford to buy him out. He supported Mom's decision to send me to the boarding school while some townsfolk were open in criticizing her. Dad did not want me to go and thought I should remain on the farm where he could teach me what I needed to know, and "What good was book larnin' at that fancy school anyway?" He thought he should be responsible for his boy, his only son. Mom and Dad disagreed so much they almost got a divorce—what Dad called splitting the blanket. Shorty told him he was wrong.

I thought of Shorty as the grocer and owner of the first implement house, which sold farm equipment, parts, and tools. Dad and Shorty got a WPA (Works Progress Administration) job hauling gravel from the creek bed to Tucumcari, where a five-and-ten-cent store was being built. Shorty drove the dump truck and saw a pretty girl in short shorts. He got so busy eyeing her that he ran that truck right up the curb and had a hard time living it down with Dad. He and Mabel were fun to be around.

Our last summer outing each year before Labor Day when I returned to school was going to the county fair. We watched fresh pink cotton candy spin onto large paper cones. We sniffed the sugary air, licked our lips, and anticipated how delicious it was going to be. Our tongues flicked out to capture delicate wisps that never disappointed.

We looked at all the exhibits. Mom entered at least one piece of needlework every year, sometimes several. She studied everyone else's pieces for quality and variety of stitching. She compared each to her work and paid attention to whose name was on it. Over time, she garnered a huge stack of first-place blue ribbons and even purple for best of show. She also was awarded red and gold ones for second and third. She acted like there was something wrong with what she had made, not quite perfect, but she was very proud to be recognized.

It was animals Dad and I sought, and Sis and I led the way to their odorous exhibits. We oohed and aahed at the strongest or cutest ones. Next came the vegetables, some huge. We dreamed how good the winning peach preserves must taste. And best of all were the rodeo and the little steam shovels where we scooped up prizes. It was a glorious adventure.

28 BRIGHT LIGHTS

No one at NMSB called attention to tasks we could not do because we had poor or no sight. The boys operated motorized and sharp equipment, and the girls made dresses and cooked. Dick was two years older and a champion typist. He was blind from birth and could type more than 125 words per minute on a portable manual typewriter, which he balanced on his lap. He was also fantastic on the piano. He played whatever songs we requested and did it hour after hour for singalongs. Four or five of us guys stood around in the music room and sang cowboy and popular hits like "Mona Lisa" and those from musicals of the day. He entertained in an Alamogordo nightclub while he was still in high school. I knew he was headed for a career as a professional musician.

Many of us walked alone, but it was natural to offer or take an arm. We were not made to feel different or handicapped or disabled. Our environment told us we would be successful.

Our teachers were good models. My teachers believed in academic excellence to prepare students for college. They challenged me to develop self-discipline and meet high goals beginning in elementary grades.

Miss Brown's voice, sometimes soft, sometimes loud, always clear, compelled me to want to please her. It was never mean or brusque. When she spoke, her tone told me she meant every word.

In her quiet, straightforward, but firm manner, Miss Brown said, "Be strong. Live life so you don't hurt others or bring shame to your families. Be truthful and do your best in everything you try. Be a good example to the younger boys and girls. Enjoy a clean life."

Miss Ruby Brown was a bright light and my favorite teacher. Her shiny hair matched her name. She made me want to be a person of good character and moral conduct. I loved and respected her because she was kind to me and everyone else. Her scent was of a pleasant floral soap. Physically large, heavyset, with thick glasses and soft hands, she patted me gently on the back, shoulder, or head. This was with kind words. She was honest. In her class, no one acted out. Very religious, she sometimes shared her faith. When she read to us, she spoke loudly and peered through a magnifier. Miss Ruby Brown dealt with low vision all her life. She came from Oklahoma like Dad's people. I heard she typed without any mistakes.

Miss Brown's weekday dresses were solid colors, grays, blues, browns, nice looking, but not classy. She wore round-toed shoes with heels about two inches high. I never saw her dressed up because we did not see teachers on the weekends. We did not eat with them either. They ate above the boys' dining room. We could hear them laughing upstairs when we left our eating area after dinner.

Mr. Harry Ditzler was an illuminator who shed light on any musical challenge. He erased fear and expanded possibilities and was my most influential music teacher. I had studied chorus with him since my first days at Alamo. As I returned to school after the summer when I was burned, I was happy to get back to the man who was president of the World Braille Music Society. He had no sight at all but taught chorus, voice, piano, and organ. He encouraged me to sing solos. I knew from afar when he was approaching.

"Mr. Ditzler must be up. I can smell his Roi Tan Cigars clear over here at the dorm," I told a roommate. I did not need any whistles or bells to tell me the time. "We better get a move on. Can't be late."

Mrs. Clalia Ditzler was fully sighted, and the couple worked as a team. She watched from the back of her husband's choral classes with a short rod in her hand.

Tap-tap-tap.

"Uh-oh." I heard the tapping sound made by the rod on a chair back and knew what that meant. Someone was misbehaving. How Mr. D knew who it was, I cannot say, but he always did, and that was not good for that somebody. He told us to begin again. Best not to have to start a third time. With receding brown hair, his balding head gave him a high forehead. The heavy eyebrows might make him look fierce, but his personality was jovial. He had a good time with people. When it came to teaching music, however, he was very serious. We gave two concerts a year with choral arrangements of classical music. Students who were not performing and townspeople were the audience.

Together, Mr. and Mrs. Ditzler earned the reputation of never having a bad word spoken about them. I thought that was an amazing accolade. He fascinated me.

"I told you about the Metropolitan Opera House in New York. I used to be a gifted singer. When I was nine, I sang there."

"Why aren't you an opera star today?"

"A young voice can be pushed too far too soon. Unfortunately, that's what happened to me. I strained my voice and did not become a professional singer."

"I'm sorry."

"Don't be, because I learned the organ, and got a fantastic opportunity. Before you came here, I once played a concert on the Mormon Tabernacle organ. You've heard recordings. It's a grand instrument."

"What was it like?" I asked.

"I'll never forget the experience. The sound was magnificent. I learned something important because a strange thing happened. As I slid across the bench, my knee hit something I didn't know was there, and I had to improvise all the way through the rest of the concert. I knew then that music was definitely my calling, so here I am."

I began to feel Dr. Quimby's influence more as I entered high school although he did not teach me in a classroom. Along with other students, I was impressed because he had a Ph.D., unusual for our community. Dr. Quimby traveled internationally to share his ideas for building a child's self-confidence and security with handicaps. He believed that confidence would spill into areas beyond athletics.

His forceful and persuasive promises echoed in my head, "Exercise will strengthen your body so you'll be less likely to get hurt throughout life."

My participation was limited at the beginning of the year as Nurse Redding dressed my leg for a few weeks. But as time passed I healed and was back to doing physical education twice a week. I tumbled and worked with the rings, climbing rope, chinning bars, parallel bars, and pommel horse. The gym coach often asked me to conduct calisthenics. I swam every Friday, wrestled, and did track and field. To run track, there were cables aligned full length on the straight surface. Leather straps were attached to the cables by small metal loops. While running, we grasped a strap and went straight ahead without encumbrances. We worked the rings to develop strength in our hands and arms. We did handstands and flips, over and over. I did the pommel horse, but totally blind fellows did not.

Despite my admiration for Dr. Quimby, he was not the main reason I enjoyed PE in ninth grade. The real reason was that I liked working with the guys, especially Paul, Tommy, and Pete. I lived with them in the senior dorm, which was on the other side of the building from the junior dorm. They were my brightest lights among peers. I met Paul when I was about eleven, but Tommy and Pete were friends from my earliest years.

Paul was a born leader, easy to look up to, an Eagle Scout, and two years older than I. He inspired us with his wit. He was my go-to-for-information man. I heard Paul lost the sight of one eye and damaged the other when he played with an ordnance he found in the desert near Las Cruces, New Mexico. Paul and I attended the Spanish Methodist church when I did not go to my Baptist one. We were put in charge of other Protestant boys from the time we got home from church till lunch. Everyone changed out of their dress suits, then had free time.

Tommy was my close brother and gave me the heart to be positive and resilient when I saw how much easier my life was than his. When he was five, Tom's face was burned severely by the explosion of a supposedly empty lye can someone threw into an open fire. That was how he lost his sight. He was gone many weeks for surgeries and got behind in his studies. I was glad each time he came back because he was cheerful and liked the things I liked. My leg had hurt a long time while it healed, so I knew he must have suffered greatly. He had a bit of light perception in one eye, but he always used braille.

My reading buddy, Pete, had no sight, was quiet, and was a good wrestler.

It was my friends I cared about, not the physical activities themselves. Bowling was the exception. The school's bowling alley was where I learned to set pins, keep score, and develop a skill I could use in sighted society as well as blind society. National competitions including the blind were beginning. I saw bowling as one of the most important parts of my education because we could bowl as well as fully sighted bowlers.

It was physically demanding to be a pinsetter but it could be thrilling. With my feet out of the way, I sat above the pit. Ten wooden pins stood at attention until a heavy bowling ball scattered them with ear-busting clatter. A pin might fly higher than my ear, hit the barrier, then drop with the others. I went into the pit, picked them up to put them into a holder, pulled a lever, and they stood ready for another strike.

Ever since the faith healer and Uncle Liston's death, I wrestled with more than boys. What did I believe about life and death, about trust and hope? Mom's faith in God was easy to see and hear. Dad considered beliefs personal and kept them private. He was uncomfortable in a church building. He honored his word, treated fellow man and animals with kindness, was a good citizen, was not a curser or a carouser, and bowed his head in respect during Mother's prayers before holiday meals and on special occasions.

I made a major personal decision to be baptized. A couple of faith-filled friends, several town kids, and a few adults also submerged in the baptistery that day, one at a time. I ascended wobbly steps from the water, silently praying please keep Mom, Dad, and Sis well, and let me see them soon. Thank you for letting me not fall in the baptistery this morning, I thought.

Aloud, I said, "You really ought to fix these steps before someone falls." The preacher was dismissive.

29 BOLOGNA AND BRAGGING

Potato salad and bologna were on the table every Saturday night from my first year at the school. I grew to hate them. The boys said a big cook mashed the potatoes with her feet. An ugly image came to my mind. Some students liked to have a food fight with the dish, but discipline was tight enough to curtail that. We sat straight and used good manners most of the time. I concentrated on not dropping things, no spills or drips. I wiped my mouth and used the correct utensil. Beautiful table manners cost me because I had to concentrate hard to cut and eat neatly. I waited to finish before talking much and did not enjoy casual conversation as most people did because I needed to focus energy to maintain neat behavior.

Nevertheless, Saturday nights with bologna and potato salad almost brought out my sloppy side until I learned to say no thank you or take only a little.

During Sunday afternoons, the girls helped the science teacher maintain the cactus garden, or we boys and girls played games by gender, read, lay out in the sun, and relaxed.

On Sunday nights, we shined our shoes out on the terraces that were around all the dorms. We separated our clothes to prepare them for the laundresses to wash and iron. The boys with some sight took turns sorting all the other guys' laundry. Ooh, boys' socks stank. I did not like that job.

Before my time, there had been a large farm where students helped raise many of the vegetables served at meals. The school used to have dairy cows to produce its own milk, and there remained a bullpen with a concrete floor and overhead cover. Its walls had ten- to twelve-inch horizontal slats with spaces between them, perfect for attaching one- and two-gallon fruit cans to hold ashes and butts. We smoked there and out at the cattle guard between the school entrance and the highway, dropping butts into the guard. We spoke in English or Spanish, combining the two into a slangy mix.

We exaggerated, made up tales, or sniggered. We shared fond memories and accusations, especially about the housemother we boys privately called *Macana*, which is a kind of short club or blackjack the Aztecs used to hit someone. Of course, she had no club, but we thought she had a harsh attitude.

We talked about how much we got away with and how we were punished when caught. Some boys said they were pinched, kicked, paddled, slapped, or shaken. I told about when I was little and practiced the Spanish I knew. I walked from the kindergarten past our building and the girls' dorm singing all my Spanish curse words, oblivious of others. I found out I had been heard when some of the kids teased me. I hoped the teachers did not hear me because I did not want to stay in my room. We all laughed at how dumb we were when we were seven, eight, nine, and how hard it usually was to get away with anything.

Another disclosure was about when I was twelve. A coach with good vision grabbed me in study hall and shook me till I thought my head would fall off. I never knew what he thought I'd done, whether I was late or what. Coach was a very big man. We boys agreed it was lucky my neck did not break. We told our tales and bragged of what strong men we became.

Even as teens, I and others were still restricted if we were caught speaking Spanish. Regardless of rules, Spanish was the language of most of my fellow students. I was confused at first and learned to say, "*No hablo español.*" Not that I needed to explain I did not speak Spanish because it was obvious. In my eight-year old mind, I knew I must learn Spanish to survive on the playground and in the dorm. Who would have guessed how much I would love it? I found myself thinking first in my adopted language despite a respectably rich English vocabulary.

In fact, Mother asked, "Do you have to use such big words in your letters? Why don't you just say what you mean?"

I thought I was, but interesting new words were added to English every year, and there were always more to learn.

Mother wrote that they got indoor plumbing. I never liked their good-humored teasing about leaving seat marks on snowy days in our drafty two-holer outhouse and did not appreciate seeing light through cracks in the walls of the tin-roofed building. I looked forward to no more bathing in galvanized washtubs.

I remembered how we thought it heaven when we acquired a Coleman lantern and could leave the kerosene or coal oil behind. They might have electricity with real lamps by the time I got home, an honest-to-goodness refrigerator, too.

30 CAUGHT BY A POSSE

A neighbor loaned me an acoustic guitar a couple of years ago. I laid the hollow body on my lap and taught myself to play it like a steel guitar because I loved Hawaiian music with its rhythm and swing. Easy listening. Easy to dance to, with messages of romance and folk tales. The neighbor eventually wanted the guitar back, so my mother ordered a steel guitar from the Montgomery Ward catalog. My new guitar was waiting when I got home.

It was a lazy summer. When Mom encouraged me to go somewhere or see someone, I told her, "I don't feel like it." When I'd start to feel sorry for myself at school, I'd think of some of Dad's stories about people who had to be courageous and go on, and I knew I had to keep trying. But it was summer, and I did not feel like trying, except with my new solid body electric guitar with its battery-operated amplifier.

I said it so many times, Mom became concerned that I was ill. I did not feel like helping. I did not feel like going. I did not feel like staying. The day she realized what I really meant was that I did not *want* to do it she came down loud and hard, waggled her index finger at me, and let me know in few words that was the last time she had better hear me say it. I had an instant turnaround.

In fact, I tried so hard to make it up to her that I cleaned Mom's new kitchen countertop. I tried to remove a tiny spot. I scrubbed and scrubbed and scrubbed, but there was still a spot. When my parents came home, they were chagrined to find a hole all the way through the linoleum.

We did not have electricity after all. It was hot. My bed was on the porch with screens to the east and south. Sometimes, I'd wake to gritty floors and sand all over my bed because a dust storm came in the night while I pulled the covers over my head. Once I awoke to Daddy's hollering. His bare foot had stepped on the cold body of a soft, dead mouse. Vines covered the east side, and we hung wet towels on the south side for cooling in the summer. Since the porch was not insulated, I would take the living room divan at Christmas, and Sis would sleep on another small bed in the corner of the same room. I liked the porch in the summer. It was airy and mine alone.

Dad and I joined a riding club called The San Jon Trail Riders. We built a small arena near town where members could rope on Sunday afternoons. Some towns called their clubs sheriff's posses. The main purpose for these clubs was to ride in grand entries and rodeo parades, which we did each night before the start of events in June, July, and August. It was patriotic with the pageantry of flags and music. The whole club wore shiny new belt buckles decorated with broncos, matching pink western shirts with pearl button studs, black western string ties, Levi's, cowboy boots, and western Panama hats of straw. Our mounts had matching breast harnesses.

That was a special time for Dad and me. And branding was special because cattlemen worked together. Branding is the way a cowboy's cattle are identified and registered. We usually branded in the spring or fall, at the same time we vaccinated the animals, dehorned them, and castrated males that would not make good breeding stock.

We built a large fire. Dad had fashioned a branding iron with his registered brand, a "reverse D heart," which he heated till red and used to burn the mark into the animal's hip or shoulder. The acrid odor of burning hair and flesh filled the air. Neighbors helped rope, hold cattle down, vaccinate, brand, keep the fire going, and watch to make sure no one got hurt. I ran from a calf, but it caught me in the behind. I flipped completely head over heels and landed on my feet, not my rear end. Cattle were red-green colorblind, so bulls were angered by movement. I must have been moving fast that day to attract his attention. Dad and I decided to eat Rocky Mountain oysters after roasting them. One bite was more than plenty.

We also broke colts, and I learned to handle them. Dad was the best horseman and blacksmith I knew, a true horse whisperer.

We rodeoed with the posse on weekends in Tucumcari, Clayton, Santa Rosa, Clovis, and Fort Sumner—all small New Mexico towns. When the rodeo was finished for one day, a friend and I met two girls my age. We asked them how far they were going. They said their transportation was about eight blocks down the road. They accepted a ride. I kicked my foot out of the stirrup and pulled one of the ladies up behind me and off we went. Dad teased me later about how that sorrel pony had never carried double before. I liked the way he did it that day.

Branding at Uncle Clyde's ranch

31 SOPHOMORE AT NMSB

As we matured, we earned free time off campus. My sight seemed to have improved a little, and my friends started calling me "Cowboy" since I dressed western. Life was good.

I was ready for more responsibility when I heard a supervisor say, "Gary, I'm putting you in charge this Saturday afternoon. I want you to take a couple of guys into town."

I was a pleased sophomore, pleased with his trust in me.

"Take my arms and let's go," I told them.

We walked the mile to town, talking about what we would do. We stopped at the café for lots of coffee and the drug store for a soda. Alamogordo was bad for having ditches running under sidewalks at intersections, so we needed to know our way around to avoid falling. I was glad to be the leader because I headed to our favorite bakery. We salivated at the mouthwatering aromas. We indulged in admiring whole pies, which sold for fifty cents apiece. We ate our delicious morsels in the park.

Whenever I led after that, we were careful. Only once did one of them step off the sidewalk into a ditch. Pretty good record.

Federal law required every eighteen-year-old man to register for the draft, Selective Service. Even total blindness did not preclude that. Before I was old enough to register, I escorted older boys, two at a time, to the downtown office so they could sign up.

On one outing, we saw the new movies *Shane* and *High Noon* for the second time. We skipped the café that day to make time for the double feature with popcorn and soda.

Another day we stopped at a carnival for the Tilt-A-Whirl, the Ferris wheel, and other rides that gave our stomachs a thrill. We did not go in the tent with the sideshow. Some people called that part the freak show. I went inside several years before. I liked the strong man but felt sorry for the bearded lady, the tiny man, the twins who were born stuck together, and the fat lady. I hated how ticket holders gawked, pointed, and made fun of people who were different. Somebody called them oddities. It seemed to me they had hard lives. I did not even want to look at the two-headed calf. I would not be part of that again.

The girls went into town in the mornings, so I did not know what they did. We boys smoked our cigarettes in town and on campus. Our movie heroes lit up, and their beautiful women blew smoke rings. From the time I was fourteen, I smoked regularly, just as all the cowboys at the rodeos back home and most of the boys at school did, even though it was against school rules.

Spending time with girls was also still taboo even though I was fifteen, but it was nice to see Liz's blonde hair in class. It was almost white. She had sight-saving special-class instruction and used enlarged print. I was in the regular class with college prep curriculum and used enlarged print, typing, and talking books. We did not see each other often before she joined my class. Liz's family home was at a pueblo west of Albuquerque, the largest city in the state. She was albino, and that was the reason for her poor vision. We became good friends and enjoyed chaperoned dances.

I wrestled with the team and went to a meet in Amarillo as a backup. The best part was that Mom, Aunt Florence, and Jo Ann came. It was a boost to see my family. As for the wrestling itself, we had meets against larger schools, such as Albuquerque High, which gave us boys a chance to travel. Although we lost some individual matches, NMSB always won its meets. Before a competition, we practiced seven days a week for one hour a day, switching partners every five to ten minutes to allow different take-down holds. We might start from a standing position or on our knees with an arm over our opponent's back. We wrestled till time was up or one would tap the mat three times because he was pinned. We finished with a two- to five-mile run.

During wrestling season, Coach monitored our weight carefully, so I ate carrots and celery till I got to the right weight. Once I got hurt when I landed on my head. My wrestling days ended in a take-down hold when my opponent squeezed me in a bear hug so hard that my nose squirted blood all over the mat. I was secretary of the athletic association, but music was more for me than physical competitions.

My friend Valentino was a savant who excelled in violin, but only in violin. He joined Lucio on the regular guitar and me on my hard body electric steel. We formed our own band and played for some of the dances.

I earned a special privilege. I loved it when an officer took me to his home at Holloman Air Force Base after he heard our matinee concert. His family treated me well and served a delicious dinner. He showed me around the base and described jobs the servicemen performed. He had a hi-fi system and asked what kind of music I wanted to hear. It was a great experience. I was glad I had practiced good table manners.

32 INTERPRETER

A big surprise came from Uncle Ralph, Aunt Mozelle's husband, when he said, "Gary Ted, I brought you some special maple so's you can build yourself a steel guitar."

The instrument I had was of soft pine and scratched easily. It did not have good sound. Dad and I used the maple and some walnut and added a bridge we made from a bone found in our fields. Maybe it was a dinosaur bone, as we did find those there, but I think it was bovine. Dad made a pattern from the Ward guitar and reused its pickup, knobs, and tuning keys. The walnut was dark brown with beautiful little striations, that showed up more when we polished it. Dad inlaid hand-cut metal frets. The walnut became the fingerboard. He decorated it with one, two, or three round slices of knitting needles among the frets. They looked like abalone. We polished the maple to a sheen. It was a fine guitar, much heavier than the old one. I bought an amplifier and enjoyed its rich sound.

I noticed the girls liked tenor voices best, so I began trying to move mine from baritone to tenor as I sang popular Hawaiian songs. I also sang a little in Spanish.

Many expressions and colloquialisms I knew used different words to refer to the same thing. Spanish-speaking students came from different places and did not all speak the same. Many of their families had lived in rural areas since before New Mexico became a state. Those from Northern New Mexico sometimes used different words than those who moved here from California or Mexico. Connotation was important. Some words packed more emotion and hidden meaning than others.

That summer, I worked in the fields. My pay was one dollar an hour, an improvement from the zero to fifty cents Dad paid. I worked as an interpreter with field hands from Mexico who came to pull golden broomcorn. It grew like wheat but was not for eating. The tassels of straw were used to make the bristles of brooms for home use. I let workers know farmers' expectations. I told the bosses what the Mexican workers required or desired in their living quarters. For instance, the pullers were used to cooking in certain ways. I translated to the bosses the number and kinds of cooking pots they told me they needed.

The San Jon area encompassed other communities. The fields at that time were around Porter and Logan. Dad remodeled the abandoned Porter schoolhouse, which had been boarded up for about twenty years. He converted classrooms to sleeping quarters and a cooking area. Ten to fifteen men slept on cots in each of the bedrooms. There were no bathing facilities. Due to strict government codes, Dad built a nearby separate humongous outhouse with about a dozen holes and screens on its windows and door. It had to be fly-proof. Even though most folks in the community had indoor plumbing by the early fifties, the building impressed me as being quite fancy for an outhouse. No matter, since I saw that many of the men stayed outside to urinate or defecate alongside the building. Of course, they used the fields while working.

Sometimes several fields were ready for gathering at the same time. The farmers instructed the pushers, or straw bosses, which fields to gather. They also supplied transportation in the back of pickup trucks, water, and food for hands to pack their own sack lunches. The hands were cooperative and wanted to work. We had no trouble. I especially recall one most imposing farmer who stood about six feet, five inches tall and packed about 225 pounds of muscle. With him around, who would dare cause trouble in his fields?

Among the pullers, some were pushers whose job was to make sure the work progressed smoothly. Pushers were group bosses who worked along with the other pullers, ensuring the crop was harvested properly and dispensed as it should be to the truck for delivery to the grain elevators. They kept order among the hands and passed on instructions from the farmers.

That was where I came in, because some of the pushers did not speak English well enough to operate on their own.

Dad knew everyone but the pullers because he had rebuilt about half the houses in the countryside and worked for many in the community throughout the season. Dad took me, his interpreter-son, to my job every day. I related well to the labor the harvesters did in the fields because I made brooms at school, where they were sold for fundraising.

I told Dad, "In a forty-five-minute shop class, I begin the broom. First, I put a pole in a vise and drill a hole near one end. I run a wire through the hole and tie it then pick up a handful of tassels. I lay them along the pole and tie them to it with the wire. I have to pull it hard and turn the pole. I keep tying on tassels all the way around the pole. Then I take longer tassels and point them in the opposite direction and keep pulling the wire as hard as I can."

"Does that hurt your hands?"

"No, but the tassels are going to be the bristles of my broom, and I don't want them to fall out when Mom sweeps hard. I bend them over to make shoulders. After I finish with the wire, I use heavy string and a needle to stitch three rows to keep the straw bristles tight. Then the teacher trims the straw so it's even."

"What's the hardest part?"

I thought a minute then said, "Holding the straw real tight and being sure it is caught."

"Ya like it?"

"Not really. Each broom takes more than one class session. The repetition is boring. I like what I'm doing in the fields a lot better. I also like construction because learning how to build makes the hard work worth it."

The hands and the bosses and Dad's contacts put me where I wanted to be. I enjoyed men's conversations and activities. The dry goods store was boring a lot of the time, but I helped Mom a little bit with Spanish-speaking customers before slipping out to Standridges' Yucca Drug. I could have a cool drink and visit with the locals to find out what was going on.

If I stayed home, sometimes Dad let me drive the pickup. I was to haul dirt he needed to put in some floors. I backed up and ran into the corner of the house, which had to be rebuilt. He gave me another chance. The last time I drove, the windshield was so mud-splashed that I had trouble seeing through it. He did not keep it clean. I got too close and ran into the back of the tractor Dad had stopped. He was still on it. I thought he would not be too proud of that, and my heart raced a little faster.

He said little, just "Hey, you ran into me."

Calmly, he checked to see if we were hung up or if the truck just bumped him. He was not unkind but said I could not drive again because he believed it was not safe. Disappointed, I guessed he did not agree with my opinion the fault was with the dirty windshield. A few lessons came harder than others.

Dad did concrete work. I helped him build a new jail, put new faces on stores when old US Rt. 66 was widened, and construct San Jon's grain elevator, theater, and several houses or outbuildings in surrounding communities. Dad and I broke for a dessert of pie and Coke every afternoon at the Beggs' Silver Grill Café when we were working in town. We really admired the pies Rose made, and a cool drink helped a lot because we did heavy labor. My favorite pie was chocolate, which she made especially for me. Without refrigerated space to keep it in the summertime, she could not sell chocolate pies, but she knew when I was coming and had mine ready in a little cooler. About mid-summer of 1953, the power company brought electricity to the café and to our farm.

Dad prepared the house for electricity. Mom went to the catalog and ordered a refrigerator and a floor lamp. When they came, it was a happy day. I realized I could bring my Talking Book machine and records the next time I came home, then thought better of it because the player without records was bulky and weighed at least fifteen pounds. It did not even have handles. Sis asked for a forty-five-rpm record player, so we could listen to popular music and Dad's favorite cowboy songs.

That Rose's pie would be waiting for me was no gamble. However, after working for Dad and in the fields a whole summer, my friends and I decided it would be fun to play poker. I knew the winning hand was going to be mine. Maybe it would be the next one. The next, or the next. That pot would be mine. It was not to be. I lost almost three weeks' wages that day and vowed never to gamble again.

Despite the apparent closeness between me and Dad, I knew he did not understand what I saw or felt. He never had. Sis was very popular all the way through school and had her own social groups and special friends. One was her high school boyfriend.

He was tall, athletic, about the most handsome fellow his age. He had a great smile and charm. Dad enjoyed taking him to shoot rabbits when I was at home. Dad was a good shot. He could pick out the eye of a squirrel in a tree from a hundred yards and not miss. I loved to go shooting. One day I used my allowance to buy ammunition, which I handed to Dad. "We can go hunting," I said. He dashed my hopes when he and my sister's boyfriend left with my ammunition and without a word of thanks.

Uncle Luther understood me much better. He was Mom's brother, a biologist, who lived in Dumas, Texas. He designed, built, and operated a lab to test tires for stretch, wear, tensile strength, and potential resistance to road hazards. The lab was part of a major company. He took me to work with him, where I saw the action. I wrote a report to take back to school. It explained where rubber came from and how it was made into the kinds of material necessary for the manufacture of vehicle tires and their tubes. Uncle Luther was my main source of information and provided samples to go with my report. The most interesting part was about the additives mixed with the rubber to give it strength. It amazed me how adding carbon black to a quarter-inch wide, four-inch long piece of raw rubber allowed the material to be stretched to four feet and rebound. I also loved listening to the local radio station DJ known as The Ding Dong Daddy of Dumas.

33 JUNIOR YEAR

Buzz went the table saw as I cut plywood to make a table top in my junior year.

"Gary," Mr. Hamilton, my shop teacher, shouted. I looked in the direction of the shout, not realizing the blade was riding right up on my flesh. My left thumb moved into the blade. Blood spurted in every direction.

"Hurry. Get him into the school car right away."

I was hustled straight to the doctor's office downtown. My thumb was sheared off to the base of the nail. A great big fat nurse sat on my shoulder to hold me down. The doctor sewed in a stitch. I rose fast and hard and pushed her off me. Back down she landed in time for another stitch. Up she went. On and on. Eight stitches pulled out before two stayed in. Whew!

That doctor did not get it quite right because that thumb had a wide tip as a result. Why didn't he give me something for the pain? I figured the doc thought it better if I stood it on my own. I learned how important it was to maintain focus when using dangerous tools.

In a strange coincidence of timing, some weeks later Dad lost much of a thumb when it caught in a cotton-rope rein attached to a hackamore on a spooked horse. A short time after that, he was using a joiner for smoothing wood. He paid no attention that his little finger slipped. He sawed it off. Both times, the tough cowboy told me there was a wild, fast car ride to be treated by a doctor. Sedatives were administered, and no one perched on his shoulder.

Over the years in shop classes, I had moved through baskets, scrub brushes, and kitchen brooms. Now I made boxes, shelves, and tables, using saws to cut the wood and the lathe to make legs. I loved woodworking. When Mr. Thomkins taught me, we made a top to play with. It was of blond oak and looked like an upside-down hot air balloon. It was flat at the broader end, so it stood when not spinning on its metal tip. I scribed six parallel lines into its midsection to hold the cord as I spun it. When we had contests, the winner's top spun longest. Mr. Thomkins was playful with our whirling creations. It was a toy to keep forever, one of the best projects I ever had.

Mr. Hamilton came after Mr. Thomkins. He and his wife were houseparents in the senior dorm. When in the stores, she insisted all her change be in crisp ones and fives that she could place in the offering plate at the Baptist church. "I'm not giving the Lord wrinkled money!" Mrs. Hamilton said.

I had come back to school my junior year with a plan. Sis would graduate in May. It was very important to me that I graduate at the same time as my twin. I had never accepted her being ahead of me as fair. I was told I could do junior and senior curricula in one year. I worked extremely hard for months to complete everything so that I would graduate at eighteen as Sis would. Then I learned that someone, somewhere, decided not to allow it, saying not enough time was spent in doing the work. Severely disappointed, I would be compelled to repeat the extra work the following year.

I dreamt I was sliding on a frozen pond during a winter that came too early. The ice said, "I'm safe." I stepped out, gained confidence, and took three steps before I heard a cracking sound and plunged into numbing cold. A heavy braille book pulled me below the surface. I tore out a single page and floated on it to the crust where Dad's lasso caught me. I let the page go. He pulled me to safety. Mom wrapped me in her homemade crazy quilt. Its warmth and bright colors woke me, and I heard myself shouting, "I will go home. I'm out of this place for good."

I fought internal battles and felt like I was in prison. Why bother to try? Wasn't there something else to life than being captive to a system that did not play in good faith? I sought identity and purpose. We heard Frank and Juanita ran off to marry. Macario whispered he would like to run home to Carrizozo, and Joseph talked about escaping to his Albuquerque home. That was not for me. Dropping out would have been deadly because I would end up back on the farm with no college and no future. What did I have at school? I was laid low and needed time to have victory over many shadows and to regain hope.

It was as if I stood on the rim of a volcano with its hot breath threatening to suck the life out of me because I found out that state law allowed me to drop out at sixteen. Of course, state law and Mom's law were not the same. Even Dad would not have wanted me to quit.

My junior year was not a loss, however, because I learned a lot while I also held a job on Saturdays at Mr. Shielie's Food Mart.

"Hey there, Archie. Could you use a stocker on Saturdays?" I asked him at church. "I sure could use the money, and I'm a good worker."

"Do you think you can do the job and be there every week on time?"

"Yes, Sir. I'd like to try."

"Come in next Saturday. We'll see if you're what I need."

I walked to work, then left at noon, walked the mile to school, ate, and walked back to work by one. I seldom missed a meal since I had a healthy appetite. Mr. Shielie liked my work sacking, carrying, and stocking goods. He paid me a regular salary and said I could work for him again during senior year.

My teacher liked my report on rubber, and my classmates felt the samples and asked questions about what I had seen.

Tommy and I spent hours listening to the radio. He put his hand on its back and acted as antenna while Matt Dillon fought outlaws on *Gunsmoke*. Sometimes, Mr. Newman invited us to listen to Jack Benny on his fine radio.

Meanwhile, Jo Ann won awards at San Jon High School and was a popular cheerleader. Her Christmas present to me had been a note that promised a box of cookies every month. No cookies came, but that was my sister. I was disappointed but not surprised.

Physically, Sis was tan like Dad, while I was fair-skinned like Mom. We differed in personality, but we were both tenacious and hardworking. Our life experiences were not similar. We had heated debates and challenging misunderstandings. From the time we were small, we disagreed on who did the most chores, who got the best gifts, or who should be allowed to go places or do things.

We often saw issues so differently that both of us became aggravated. During several periods, we vacillated from staying completely apart to sticking together. Generally, we got along well between disagreements and had good times. However, Sis told me I was "disowned" more than once. Maybe we each thought the other was headstrong and ourself right.

In good times, Jo Ann said she admired how my brain worked and how I could see beyond a situation, whereas she took things at face value. She said I made connections and figured out just about anything. School was her element, not mine. We differed in expectations and in how we proceeded to realize goals. We had diverse challenges, but her sight was intact. We never directly discussed how she felt about my living at the school, but I thought we had a lot of sibling rivalry.

Dad and Sis picked me up in May, and we drove to visit Granddad Sam Montague. We listened to the radio program *Truth or Consequences* on the way. I heard Granddad was exceptionally strong when young. Dad told stories about how Granddad and Uncle Ed could pick up an engine block and put it in place alone. Now he was in his twilight years. He lived in humble lodgings along the banks of the Rio Grande near Hot Springs, New Mexico. Daddy's father had left Granny after two children died before maturity. His ten other children were on their own. He chose to follow in the way of a separatist religious sect, positive he knew God's one path to Truth. He never again became a real part of our larger family.

Sis was going to marry her tall, handsome, and athletic beau as soon as she graduated. She talked about her plans to go to college while he was in Okinawa with the military. They would have only two weeks together before he left. He would be gone more than a year. She asked me to sing at the wedding. Our good friends Tommy Jo and John joined me. I believed Jo Ann thought she would live happily ever after. That made me share her joy. They seemed young but a good match.

I continued to interpret in the fields. It was a job that fit me perfectly.

Loneliness remained a problem. I did not have close buddies, and I felt excluded by other fellows. They had grown into strangers with their own busy activities, physical abilities, and close friendships. They drove pickup trucks and were independent. Whenever I saw Bill and Jackie or Sonny, they would play a prank to see if I knew them. I always identified each one by his voice.

I rode into San Jon with my parents every few days, but one day I stayed home and then decided to walk the three miles along the side of Route 66. Road noises confused me. Speeding vehicles made me nervous. My parents chewed me out and told me I had to be more careful. They need not have worried, as I wanted never to repeat the experience.

When they brought me to town, I ran across Route 66 to the Implement House where Bill worked. It was a major two-lane highway. There were no signs reducing speed through town, but cars tended to slow a bit as they saw the six blocks of buildings. I was confident the San Jon sheriff was somewhere nearby. I listened for road noise to determine speed and watched for glint and glare off vehicles. Local drivers turning onto the highway were considerate. I was used to running on sidewalks at school and competing in track, so I was sure footed.

Sometimes I ran back across to help Mom in the store, especially on days when field hands were paid. She might need an interpreter. When there were no customers, she reminisced. She said her daddy never forced the younger girls to work the way she had.

"I was so happy to meet Mayrene Campbell when I was thirteen. We were close like sisters. Mayrene's family had much more than we did, but they were sharing people. I wanted to go to high school in Tulia, Texas, so I boarded with the Campbells. Did you know I used to be so good and fast at softball that my classmates called me a wildcat player?"

"Never heard that before."

"Mayrene and I graduated together, and you know we're still close. I sewed well and made my own graduation dress with rows and rows of ruffles. I was tickled. I'll show you a picture sometime. I was happy with the Campbells." She became quiet.

"What happened after you got out of high school? Did you stay with Mayrene?"

"After graduating from high school, life was not as comfortable as it was when I lived with them. Mayrene went to college and became a teacher. I moved back to Plainview, Texas, and into a boarding house run by Mrs. Myrtle Montague."

"Granny?"

"Yes. She was my landlady, which meant I paid her rent for a room and meals. I went to work at the five and dime. I worked ten-hour days, six days a week, and I only got eight dollars for the whole week. That boss at F. W. Woolworth would not allow employees to sit down anytime during the day. Can you imagine what that's like? I got so tired my bones ached."

"Did Dad live at Granny's, too?"

"Yes, that's where we met. His name, of course, was really Grant Thomas Montague, but everybody called him Tood. Don't know how that got started. He fixed everything that broke. He was handsome. He called me a classy lady."

Mother tilted her head. Had she blushed?

"We married, and I found a new job keeping books for a nice man who ran a small business. I liked that job. We were proud I didn't have to stand all day. We were happy. After almost nine years we moved from Plainview, Texas, to Tres Piedras, New Mexico. We were going to homestead on open land the government made available."

"Was it expensive?"

"It didn't cost anything if we agreed to live on it and make improvements. We looked forward to having our own place. We were going to raise animals and crops. Tood told me the countryside was beautiful with tall pines and shorter piñón trees. And he was right."

"Did you know anybody there?"

"No, but your Aunt Florence and Uncle Red were going, too, and we would live near each other. We got along so well with them and were excited to be starting out on our own land."

She described our little house with dirt floors she swept and how she continued to keep freshly ironed linens on the table even after she added washing diapers for two outside on the washboard to her daily chores. "I had very little time for sewing and reading, but I managed to stitch and crochet clothes for you young'uns and read the Bible."

It was a well-thumbed Bible.

"I picked and sold piñon nuts. Your dad labored hard all day, every day, working the soil, caring for the animals, and building what we needed. Sometimes I envied my sister Florence for having it easier, caring for her husband Red and not working like I did."

That's how I felt about Jo Ann.

Mom went on, "I had to ask God to forgive me because He says it's not right to covet what someone else has, and that's what I was doing."

I got the message not to envy others. It was with family history, mixed emotions, and a heavy heart that I boarded the train for my last year at NMSB. At that moment, I hated school and did not look forward to another year of study. Why was this happening to me? I did not want to go to college, either. Mother said her friend Mayrene, the teacher, insisted I must.

34 GOODBYE TO ALAMO

Mom had told me what she thought might have caused my vision loss, and I began to wonder about some of the other students. A few, like Tom and Paul, had accidents. Some had an illness. My optic nerves did not develop beyond the stage of infancy. In some families, several children were albino. My state had three blind people per thousand, the highest rate in the nation, but that was from all causes in the broad range of visual impairment.

I did some research and found the school began as the Asylum for the Deaf, Dumb and Blind in Santa Fe in 1893 in the Territory of New Mexico. It was an expansion of the Asylum for the Deaf and Dumb, established in 1887. The 1900 census showed sixty-eight blind people of school age in New Mexico. It was hard to get the blind to come to the Santa Fe asylum, so a land grant and legislative funding in 1903 established the New Mexico Institute for the Blind at Alamogordo. Classes began in 1906 with twenty-one students.

New Mexico became a state in 1912 and, of the continental states, had been the last to establish a school for the blind. From 1925 to 1954, it was named the New Mexico School for the Blind. When I was almost ready to graduate, it became the New Mexico

School for the Visually Handicapped (NMSVH). I thought that was progress because the name indicated not all of us were totally blind, even though we did not use the word *handicapped* at school or in my family.

I learned that the infant mortality rate was higher in New Mexico than in most states. More babies died from all causes in my state than in any other in the whole country. I wondered why. Some people said parts of our population had low health standards. Syphilis caused a few vision problems. Back when I was born, there were modern sewage treatment plants in only seven cities in New Mexico and a lot of people who were poor.

By my senior year, New Mexico still had many poor people. Some NMSVH students did not have good diets at home. A few could see better after a year or two of good nutrition at Alamo. They went home to public school. I became aware that some of our students did not go home at Christmas because their parents could not afford the train or bus fare. That was worse than all the years Mom and Dad missed my events. I did not know what brought each student to the campus, but I did learn that some came by themselves without even a mother to tuck them in the first night.

Several things pushed me to grow up fast. One was being the butt of bullying on and off the school grounds. When some of my completely blind classmates and I went to the movie theater a year or two before, we heard a few town kids taunt us.

"Look! See the idiots from the asylum!"

They must have known what the first school was called. While I might see differently than others, I was determined to be treated on a par with those of the sighted world.

When I first arrived at school, I did not know up from down about anything. With one train ride, my life changed forever. Losing everything familiar overwhelmed me. I felt as far from home as I think it possible to feel and quite alone. I did not know if I should be ashamed to be sent away. I was confused and had to adjust. It seemed cruel to make me leave home suddenly at eight years of age. I did not think it was necessary. I did not agree with Mom's decision.

Over the years, I developed into an independent person in charge of my own destiny. Even though most of each year was spent in Alamogordo, home was on the farm with Mom, Dad, and Sis. The school staff reinforced that from the beginning. They did not usurp my family while serving in its place during student performances, athletic competitions, and decision-making.

My temperament was such that I think if I had stayed at home, I would have exploded with frustration, maybe become violent, at the desire for independence. Mom knew this about me. I began to understand myself and how fortunate I was. I turned my mind toward my band, chorus, shop, studies, and Liz. I began to accept my situation, like Miss Brown and Mom must have done in the past. I changed my focus and appreciated what I had.

Academics and music instruction at NMSVH were outstanding. I liked all my violin teachers over the years: Miss Clark, Miss Harden, Mr. Kaminsky, and Miss Rickel. Edwina Rickel, another bright light, was genteel, an instrumentalist and vocalist extraordinaire. I discovered the music of a singer named Patrice Munsel. Miss Rickel's soaring soprano clarity made me happy and carried my mind to joyous rendezvous with Patrice Munsel in heavens unknown.

Our student body changed over time. We had a greater number of students who had multiple difficulties, and I helped them because my only problem was limited eyesight. Perseverance led me to excel in daily living skills, which some of them needed help to learn, and I liked to do what I could to guarantee their success.

School discipline seemed less rigid during my senior year. More freedom was nice, but some students took advantage and argued with coaches and others. It did not help that coaches came and went. Agitators stirred up problems. The days of forcing students into a mold were passing. Some kids had had enough of rules and acted out just to be acting out, like when they slammed apples against the wall outside the dining hall rather than eat them.

In shop, I learned skills that I shared with Dad to make his job easier. He decided education was worthwhile and was not the fancy schooling he had ridiculed when I was younger.

At 5'10-1/2" and a senior, I became enraged at the teacher we privately called *Tecolote* (owl) for the large dark-rimmed glasses he wore. He grabbed me. I pushed back. *Tecolote* fell down the stairs. I also fell. At the bottom, I offered to go to the office with him, probably with an I-dare-you attitude, but the teacher would not go. Luckily, graduation was coming soon. I was ready.

Such treatment rarely happened to me, but it was hard to forgive when I felt it unjustified. Maybe its purpose was to further my desire for independence and a normal life. I decided to go to Albuquerque to attend college.

Uncle Luther, Mother's brother, was the only one from either side of my family who was a college graduate. He taught me that the reason to go to college was to learn where to find information, and that was what I was looking for.

Even Dad agreed I should go. I saw Audie Murphy in *Ride Clear of Diablo* and thought about my horse. Dad sold my Diablo and gave me forty silver dollars. I loved Diablo especially but would not need him at college. We still had Ball-ee and Zephyr at home.

Many of our students graduated at twenty-one or twenty-two years old, but I had just turned nineteen. NMSVH had eighty-eight students when I graduated in 1955. Four were in my senior class. Liz, from a Native American pueblo, and Gus, from a Roswell farm, went home after graduation. Joe, from Mora, and I went to the University of New Mexico.

My folks bought my class ring and a graduation suit for Liz. I paid for her class ring.

By my graduation day, Jo Ann had completed a full year at a small college in northern New Mexico. I looked forward to what was coming next for me.

Miss Brown shook my hand and said, "God bless you, Gary. Do good things in the world. Make us proud."

Miss Rickel dazzled me with her smile and warmth and reminded me to make beautiful music.

My math teacher, Mr. Newman, peered through his large dark-rimmed glasses and congratulated me for setting out to do more than build fence.

Dr. Quimby said nice things about all of us, and Mrs. Quimby assured us we would succeed in life.

Best of all, Mom, Dad, Sis, Aunt Florence and Uncle Red, and Dad's business partner from San Jon came for the ceremony. My heart was filled with hope for success, meeting challenges, and love. I sang three solos. "Give a Man a Horse He Can Ride" said I could be happy with simple things and use all I had learned for what I needed to do. "Climb Every Mountain" encouraged me to follow my dream no matter what obstacles arose. "Charity" reminded me that love is the most important thing in life.

I had ached for my family to come until I was almost numb, but they had heard none of my other concerts. We shared a poignant, proud moment.

With the diploma from the New Mexico School for the Visually Handicapped in hand, I was ready to tackle my next challenge at the largest university in the state. It was the only one I considered attending because it was the hardest, and I refused to settle for anything less.

35 TESTING MY METTLE

After an eye exam, the cabbie dropped me at a First Street hotel, where I struggled to sign a traveler's check. I was in Albuquerque because the New Mexico Division of Services for the Blind required eye and aptitude tests to qualify me for UNM. A bare bulb glowed above a single high bed in my room. I went to the commode and tin-walled shower down the hall. The water was barely warm.

As I set out for breakfast the next morning, shots rang out.

"Whoa! What the…?" I froze, praying to be invisible.

When a policeman approached, I asked for directions. He shoved me against a wall and demanded to know who I was and why I was there. When I told him, he believed me and let me go. After the aptitude test, I inquired at banks and companies about job openings and had several good interviews. Businessmen said, however, that my limited sight made it impossible for them to hire me.

My first trip to Albuquerque ended, and I went home to do summer work with Dad.

For so long, it had been a mystery why my family had not

come for special events at Alamo. I decided to ask. Mom went to her desk for a packet.

"Son, here are the letters you and your teachers wrote when you were little. You had to dictate until you could write braille well, so the teacher typed them. Every time you begged us to come, tears rolled down my cheeks."

"Sometimes I cried, too." A lump hurt my throat.

"I'm sure you never told us that, but once you said you tried not to cry for us. I bawled like a baby and wanted to come hear you sing and meet all your teachers. It was a long, expensive trip. I had the store, and crops and animals depended on your dad."

"We gave fine concerts. You would have loved the music. I sang solos and—"

Mom interrupted, "Son, that's not why we stayed away to begin with. Do you remember Mrs. Cole?"

How could I forget my first teacher at Alamo? I read what Mrs. Cole wrote during the first month I was there:

I know that you miss Gary but try to comfort yourself by knowing that he is much better off in a school of this kind by really going to school and learning, which is the natural thing for any mother to want for her child. Do feel free to write us as often as you wish and come to see us when you feel that you can.

Only one month later, she typed:

Oct. 25, 1944.

We teachers for the blind certainly enjoy an understanding mother, and I know you are one. Please rest assured that everything possible is being done for your boy. I think, and hope, that you will be very proud of him when you again see him.

I do not think it would be wise for you to visit Gary now as it would only make him homesick again when you left. He seems to be quite adjusted to his surroundings and is very content with your letters of encouragement, and your packages, and the anticipation of your coming, which I hope you can continue to "put off" for a while by writing that you are just too busy.

It took Gary a full month to adjust himself to the fact that he must learn braille. He still wants to use his eyes, so for the past two weeks I have kept an apron over his hands. He doesn't like this apron, so now he is showing me that he does not need it. Our bargain is that as soon as he uses his eyes when reading and writing braille, he must use an apron over his hands again.

I think sometimes he daydreams about home and his fingers just refuse to talk for him. This all takes time so don't worry—all we need is plenty of patience.

Mrs. Cole wrote my words of invitation in my letters home. How could she do that while at the same time she told them to pretend to be too busy? By the time I read her December 1944 letter where she again thanked Mother for being understanding and not visiting, I wanted to find that woman and tell her what I thought of her.

"But, Mom, it was eleven years. Why didn't you come after I adjusted?"

"At first, we were afraid we would set you back. We wanted the best for you, Gary. Leaving you there was worse than picking cotton for my father. Tougher than living on the homestead. You seemed to be getting along well, and there was nothing for you in San Jon schools. I guess it was easier not to upset your progress. After a while, it became a pattern."

36 GREENHORN

A few weeks later, my well-traveled rawhide suitcase and I arrived at Mesa Vista Dormitory at UNM and found no rooms available. I bunked uneasily in the basement with ten or fifteen men, mostly older military fellows returning from Korea, and found I had missed supper. I learned there was a catalog.

The next morning, I joined an orientation meeting so full that I stood at the back of the room and had trouble keeping up with the presentation. Something was written on the board. People scattered when the first meeting ended a couple of hours later. I got lost and missed the next presentation but picked up a catalog that listed all the classes.

Sis worked in Albuquerque and read the catalog to me after work. I confirmed my schedule the next day, looked for class locations, and found several were to meet in different buildings or classrooms than listed. The bookstore was next. Some texts were in stock. Others were not. There was no buddy system. I disliked floundering and fought the urge to go home, but life improved when I got a dorm room.

Having no recorded books jarred me more than I expected. I struggled to take notes fast enough and to read printed texts with a hand-held magnifier. Sis and I developed a plan. Six days a week, I hiked twenty-seven city blocks from UNM to meet her at a downtown finance company at 7:00 p.m. Then we walked a dozen blocks to her apartment. She read textbooks to me before I set out on late, fearful treks to the dormitory. One night, a dark Chevy approached slowly.

"Want a ride, Buddy?"

I climbed in. Off we headed. The driver placed his hand on my knee and moved it up my thigh. I wanted to park him one.

"You stop this car right now. Let me out immediately," I demanded.

He slammed on the brakes. Over the next few weeks, I kept seeing that Chevy approach me at intersections.

Despite difficulties, I was in general studies classes by 8:00 a.m. every day. I was the first freshman with low vision welcomed into the University Chorus. While other students held sheet music, I worked to memorize everything during class. I needed a tape recorder.

Away from campus, I made friends with several managers of state-run snack bars and earned spending money by working part time.

Back on campus, UNM did not know what to do with me for physical education. I thought modern dancing sounded like a good choice. I could make use of all those steps I learned at Alamo, the turkey trot, schottische, and *Put your Little Foot*. Instead, I heard something like ballet music and saw bare feet, flowing skirts, and bright scarves. The professor explained we were to express our innermost feelings through extreme physical movement. She was a free-spirited woman whose long, gray hair sailed as she twisted and leapt wildly across the gymnasium, imitated by the rest of the class who were female gazelles. I transferred to calisthenics.

The academic load and time it demanded were crushing. I was mortified to fall behind and knew Sis would leave town at the end of the school year. I finally found my Alamo friend, Paul, and asked, "How do you do it, Paul?"

"I've still got a little sight in one eye and read textbooks and maps. Smile a lot, and people will help you." He understood my situation. "You need to go to the dean's office."

I took Paul's advice and met Miss Elizabeth Elder from the dean's office. She brought the cavalry to save me. Town Club, an independent university sorority for Albuquerque women students, took me on as a service project in the second semester. The first TC readers, Patricia and Betty, met me in the hazy dining room of the Student Union Building, the SUB, which reeked of tobacco and bacon. Clattering china cups, conversation, and laughter competed with the treatises of authors and soft-voiced coed readers. I had trouble hearing and concentrating.

In class, one professor's voice did not project enough to be captured by my new sixty-pound Wilcox-Gay tape recorder with seven-inch reels. It was heavy to carry but it was worth it as I could replay the lecture at night. When a screw fell out and was lost, Don of Sigma Chi left campus to buy what I needed and refused payment. Such a small gesture for a sighted person but a gift for me. Don also read to me in the dorm.

Most other readers did not help during test week, but Carol read only for tests. Some of the ladies talked about boyfriends, but most were serious about covering the material. A few standouts held me to task and identified salient points. A couple were study-buddies who shared notes. It was hard on me to get only partway through, so the TC women did their best to read all my materials while preparing for their own classes.

Although much better with readers, school was never smooth. I retained most information by hearing, but it was difficult to listen to some voices no matter how well-intentioned the readers were.

37 JUGGLING NEEDS WITH PROFESSORS

Sophomore year began in an off-campus apartment with three fellows, two from home and a stranger named John. Robert and I were studious. Not the others. Disagreements erupted. Robert had a high-fidelity system and a .45 caliber pistol. He was timid. I encouraged him to stand up to a bully in one of his classes, and I even protected him. All of us disagreed on who could turn on the hi-fi. Sharing meal preparation duties failed. John made rude remarks about everything, including religion, so I judged him to be wacko. I felt unsafe after a month when three of us got into a fist fight. I moved back to Mesa Vista Dorm. Soon after, Robert shot his gun to scare John, but the bullet hit John's arm. They moved back to the campus and dispersed. I no longer cared.

I had professors to handle. An intractable one said, "You will take my test the same as the other 200 students in your class. You have one hour and will bubble in your answer. Either you can do it, or you can't."

I was drowning because taking notes without seeing the chalkboard was taxing enough without fighting the testing style. Howard Metheny, Dean of Men, intervened by telling the professor, "You need to be reasonable. He cannot possibly read all those questions in the time others can. He needs for you to let him take an oral exam."

Dean Metheny also told me, "You keep me posted by giving the OK sign with your thumb and middle finger when you pass my office." An uneasy truce existed while I finished the course, and the professor assigned a teaching assistant to test me orally.

Most instructors had a trait that made me remember them. Understanding professors like Dr. Sasaki had no problem with my bringing a reader. He had lived in the crowded housing of a World War II Japanese Internment Camp for Americans of Japanese heritage, where the food was not like that at his home. A professor of sociology, he talked with me before and after class. In private conversations, he shared feelings about the prejudice he had faced after World War II, but he never brought it up in class.

As the year ended, senior readers graduated, but most of the others continued, and Town Club sent new pledges. Each semester, I also had a few readers from a men's service fraternity, two other social sororities, and two honor societies. Town Club sent about thirty girls every semester. There were also large community-minded organizations that recorded books upon request, but recordings arrived on flimsy disks or too late.

I felt simultaneously excited and anxious when I finished general studies and declared for entry into the College of Education. A board of five university professors and administrators convened to interview applicants with physical limitations. There was a fellow in a wheelchair and another with a wooden leg and crutches. The woman before me cursed as she stomped out of the interview room. She said she was denied but given no reason. She was nicely proportioned but only a little over four and a half feet tall. I was next to be questioned.

"How will you maintain discipline without good eyesight?"

I explained how I would use voice control, both volume and tone, move about the classroom, lay a gentle palm on a shoulder, talk quietly with an individual, give a troublemaker a way to contribute to the class, offer extra help outside of class, and set clear expectations.

When I was approved, the dean of the college said, "You may get into this college, but you will never teach in Albuquerque Public Schools."

He cast the glove at my feet. I ran the gauntlet with spirited determination.

I found fewer readers during summer school and wished the university would match volunteers to those in need. The struggle of a low-vision student was not obvious to others. It took me as much time preparing to study—getting access to textbooks and course material on time and in a form that I could use—as studying. I wished for large print, recordings, and a quiet place. I completed my courses but resolved to work at home the next summer.

In the fall, I moved into "OK Corral." It was a recycled World War II Quonset hut used as a dormitory for only that year. Each of us had our own room and got along well. Lindy, dignified and highly moral, studied accounting. He was closest to me. Steve, a Hungarian Revolt refugee, was an artist. Ryan was a meticulous record keeper. Louie, a slight fellow with blond hair, invested in gold mines and had a hand so steady I watched him use a woodcut freehand to print cloth for curtains. Big Mike, ex-Navy, 240 pounds, five feet eight inches, started college at age thirty-five, studied journalism, and barhopped. Mike and Louie had cars and offered transportation. I admired the woodcarvings and other art that Arthur brought from his home in Taiwan. Our last occupant, Walt, had been in trouble at an engineering school and transferred to UNM. He told big tales of wild parties, guzzled a lot of beer, and decorated his windowsill with bottles.

Mother's letters came once a week, like they always had. She said my cousin had returned the little violin, my first, but it was damaged. The back was cracked, and it needed other repairs. I knew that meant it was unplayable. Had my overactive young cousin used it to hit a brother or sister? Weren't my aunt and uncle going to pay to fix it?

Meanwhile, my social life was up and down. Liz adored Marty Robbins, so I took her to his outdoor concert on campus. We stood close to the stage where the small man with big feet and an even larger voice performed "Ghost Riders in the Sky" and "A White Sport Coat and a Pink Carnation" as he flirted with ladies in the audience. I decided he was too friendly with my girl, so I led her away, afraid I would pop him one. Before long, religion came between Liz and me. I told her I was Baptist and could not become Catholic. She was Catholic, would not become Baptist, and got furious. We broke up.

At UNM, several readers became close friends. I had coffee dates with two sisters and was attracted to one, but it did not go anywhere. Nancy was another favorite. One gal hung around me a lot, but she was not a good student. I asked Patricia out, but she said, "Definitely not." After that, I did not ask any of the readers except Nancy. She and I planned to celebrate her twenty-first birthday. But when she married a tall blond intellectual in one of her classes, she changed her mind about going out with me.

Virginia and I met at a meeting of the National Federation of the Blind (NFB). She was the secretary for the city manager. We walked or traveled by bus. I used a monocular to figure out which buses to take but I sometimes missed them. It was on one of our walks that Virginia ran into a post and hurt her head. I felt terrible that I had not seen that post. Her tear ducts would not let her cry, but they felt better when I put in drops. She had glass eyes and had been a registered nurse before diabetes took her sight. Attractive and poised, Virginia was a smart dresser and good cook. We met after church to go to her parents' home, where I was the burger chef. We had movie, food, and soda dates, played Hawaiian music on her phonograph, danced, and snacked on popcorn. My dad made a checkerboard for her, the kind with depressions for handmade checkers. On a car ride from an NFB meeting, she sat on someone else's lap, and afterward our relationship cooled. She said she was proud of what I had accomplished, but she was hoping to find a sighted husband. I was shattered about the deterioration of our relationship because she was a fine person.

My reader and friend, Betty, lived in Hokona Hall, the women's dorm. We arranged to see each other at a Christian youth meeting. She brought a freshman from the dorm, Elaine Carson, who smiled at me with her Shirley Temple smile. She had the movie star's curls, too. Betty introduced us later during the party in the minister's campus home.

"Do you believe in ESP?" Elaine asked.

"Extra sensory perception, the ability to become aware of things by something beyond our normal senses, seems probable to me," I replied.

"What about space travel? What do you think about going to the moon and maybe even colonizing Mars?"

I did not spend a lot of time thinking about colonizing space, but I knew that in the past Europeans did not think of settling the American continent because they did not know it existed. Couldn't it be the same for outer space?

"Let's get our tickets," I said.

"Well, if someday we can travel on a spaceship, maybe beings from other worlds have come here. What about that?"

Only a decade had passed since the Roswell incident about space aliens landing in New Mexico. Since many civilizations had disappeared, could the mystery of aliens settling on Earth bear some truth?

As our conversation moved from ESP to outer space in the span of a few minutes, we were unaware of anyone else in the room until I walked the girls to their dorm. Elaine and I made a date for the next night. Then we sat in a drugstore booth for the next thirty consecutive nights and talked without running out of topics. We drank hot tea or coffee on alternating nights to learn to enjoy what the other preferred.

"Would you like Dentyne?" I pulled the red foil pack of small bricks from my pocket. Dentyne was Dad's favorite gum and turned out to be hers and her dad's, too. We had a lot in common. We were both surrounded by beautiful pop, classical, operatic, and liturgical music as we grew up. Our religious faiths and outlooks coincided.

As Elaine talked of growing up in a military family and living on bases, I shared pleasant memories of being a guest in the homes of officers after concerts. She did not tire of hearing about the farm and my school.

She said, "I've been to the rodeo. I shook hands with Roy Rogers and Dale Evans at the State Fair rodeo. Do you ride?"

She knew nothing about the importance of rodeos to small western communities or how they demonstrate the skills cowboys need on the range. I told her about events, parades, and the music and dancing at barn dances. For me, Roy Rogers and Dale Evans were on the silver screen on Saturdays.

"When I was about 11, my family was at an outdoor rodeo in the middle of nowhere," she said. "A bull broke loose and burst out of the arena. Everyone ran for cover. Riders corralled him before anyone got hurt, but it scared me. To tell the truth, I don't like to ride horses much as I'm not comfortable around such big animals and think I might fall." She sounded reluctant to admit not liking farm animals, like maybe I would be disappointed.

"Not everyone is. I grew up with horses and learned to understand them. But I don't like every horse either." I told her about ours and the little Shetland Dad taught to pull a cart with his grandchildren inside.

She described the antics of her seven-year-old brother and how close they were. She explained her father was an intelligent nuclear scientist who made stern rules but who was loving. Her mother was a homemaker who volunteered at the hospital and in the community. I spoke of Mom's store and cowboying and building with my dad. Visitors left calling cards on silver saucers at Elaine's home, and some arrived in full dress uniforms with swords at their sides. Our families were very different.

Elaine and I were hooked and didn't look back. I met her parents at Sunday dinner in their home. Her mom was an excellent cook and took to me right away. It was not the same with her dad, a full bird colonel in the Air Force. He was polite, cautious, and friendly but distant. I noticed a coffee service on a sideboard and commented I'd not seen a gold set before. We came many more Sundays, and I saw it had been polished and gleamed silver once the tarnish was removed.

Shortly before the 11:30 p.m. closing time as we returned to campus, we found an unsettled crowd, mostly males, gathered near the front of Hokona Hall dormitory. We were dressed in our Sunday best, in sharp contrast to demonstrators who crowded both sides of the long sidewalk that led to the entrance steps. I held Elaine's arm firmly.

"Go directly to your room. Lock the door, and don't open it. Do it right now," I told her.

She went inside. I turned to face the agitators and started down the steps. The crowd pressed closer but moved back from the walkway, parting like the Red Sea. It was amazing the way they stepped aside for me.

In my dorm room a block away, I waited anxiously with no phone. I learned that a few UNM students demanded a vacation day because the UNM Lobos had defeated the Arizona Wildcats thirty-three to thirteen. They built a bonfire outside President Popejoy's house. Three times they demanded. Three times he refused because it was a holiday week. They burned him in effigy and marched to Hokona. The crowd grew to several hundred. The agitated group stormed the girls' dorm only a few minutes after we had arrived and made off with panties, bras, sweaters, clocks, jewelry, radios, and cameras. They ran through Elaine's wing moments before she got there, damaging windows, screens,

and doors. Her terrorized roommate refused to let her in at first.
The City Safety Director called the panty raid mob violence. The
Fire Chief was assaulted, a police car was damaged, and panties
flew from the flagpole the next day.

This occurred on our normally peaceful 1958 campus while
we heard about other parts of the country, such as Arkansas,
Virginia, and Louisiana, where authorities responded to civil
rights protests by closing high schools to resist integration. That
was not a problem at UNM.

In November, we went to the Sandia Mountains to picnic
with my parents. Mom brought fried chicken and chocolate
cake all the way from the farm. Dad taught Elaine how to play
mumbly peg, a game where we flipped a pocketknife.

On our dates, Elaine and I walked or rode the bus to campus
activities and dances. We ordered thin-crusted pepperoni pizza
at Casa Luna. Sometimes we double dated, but we did not need
other people or lots of hubbub because we enjoyed being together
by ourselves.

"Do you like what I'm wearing?" she asked one day.

"You could wear a burlap sack, and I would like it."

Next day, we were in the dorm recreation room alone. She
removed her coat to reveal she was dressed in a burlap bag! I
picked her up and spun her around as we laughed.

As the school year progressed, Elaine became a Town Club
member, and we talked of marriage. Some dormmates she barely
knew came uninvited to grill her one night.

Elaine reads to Gary at UNM Student Union Building

"Why would you get serious with a guy who can't see well and is poor? You better find out what caused his problem and what kind of family he comes from. What if you have children?"

Elaine was shocked at their insinuation that only trouble could come of it. She did not tell me about them right away but decided to quit the university at the end of the year to get business training.

"Are you sure you want to do that?" I knew she was a scholar at heart.

"I don't see how we can marry when you graduate next year unless I have a job."

"Okay. But be sure that's what you want to do. What will your folks say?"

"Don't know."

"How're you going to tell them?"

We knew we would have a wonderful future together, but I did not think her parents would welcome her news.

While Elaine lived with her parents the next year and with OK Corral torn down, I had a single room at the new Coronado Dorm when I was a senior. It was at the end of a hall near an exit leading to a second-floor deck. It was a great place to live, but I locked my door when I heard guys throw glass bottles in the hall. Sounds of a vending machine crashing down the stairwell came next, then campus cops.

A new SUB opened. Dorm friend Jethro managed the building and gave me a key to a private room for reading. That made studying significantly easier. The reading room was bright. An interior glass wall adjoined a busy hallway. I did not mind being seen until a reader wore a mini-skirt that rode up high. I threw my jacket over her knees and commented, "This'll cut down on viewers." After that, she wore slacks.

Another reader always sat far from the table with her legs carefully crossed at her knees. Patty was president of Town Club and made sure I had all the readers I needed.

Some liked to stand. "Early man left his mark in the dense canyon of—" Bang onto the floor went the text. Kerplop into a chair went the girl. My reader that day had walked while reading anthropology and fell asleep under its spell.

About the same time, I was filled with satisfaction when I made the last payment to Sears for my new twenty-pound Wollensak seven-inch reel-to-reel tape recorder. It was a lot lighter to carry.

One midday, I called the business school and told Elaine to come to the university right away because a package had arrived. She was so excited that she brushed aside a girlfriend who had come to have lunch with her, ran to the bus, and rushed into the reading room. At age twenty-three, I placed an engagement ring upon the finger of my nineteen-year-old fiancée. She took her breath in sharply and hugged me tight as she admired the ring.

"Is it a real diamond?" she asked.

"Let's see. Diamonds will cut glass. Give me your hand."

We made a tiny scratch on the glass of the reading room and were satisfied.

Even though she was working instead of attending classes, Elaine showed up at a Monday night Town Club meeting, and the girls were not surprised. It was stylish to wear short gloves even when it was not cold, so they did not suspect anything when she wore them. The meeting was about to end when the president said, "Let's form the Town Club circle because we have a Candlelight Ceremony tonight."

Elaine told me the president lit a beautiful turquoise and gold candle, and the girls passed it from person to person around the circle. Quizzical looks flashed among the excited girls while Elaine said she tried to keep a poker face, so they could not guess it was her candle. Every girl passed it, and the candle started around again. That told them no one was going steady or pinned, which meant making a commitment by accepting a boyfriend's class ring or fraternity pin. Some of the girls pretended to blow the candle out but stopped short of exhaling and passed it on. If it went around three times, someone was married. But the candle did not make it three times. When it came to Elaine on the second circuit, she extinguished the flame to say that she was engaged. A commotion of congratulations erupted. She said the girls, most of them my readers, were very happy for us. They told me themselves the next day.

Not too long thereafter on a winter night I left Elaine's home and searched for the gate of the military base. I had trouble because it was snowing. I'm going to freeze before I get there, I thought, wishing her father had offered me a ride. He never did that. Was he trying to show her how adequate or inadequate I was and whether I could take care of her? I knew I could but felt I needed to prove it to him. I guess fathers are like that about daughters.

On a more pleasant night a couple of months later, I walked confidently across a grassy area. Without warning, I fell into a newly-dug trench in an unlit field that I had crossed many times before. I held on to the edge while my feet dangled. I dug my fingers into the dirt as I tried to climb from the trench. Disoriented and hurting all over, I struggled out and heard a motor. If a soldier had not given me a ride to the base gate, I never would have caught the last bus for the night.

38 PRACTICUM, STUDENT TEACHING

In my last semester, I invented a heated bus stop where I could wait Monday through Friday. A speaker informed me when each bus arrived and where it was going. Coffee was handy and steaming, and the cup kept my fingers warm. The problem was that my invention and the cup were both only in my imagination.

I pulled my sport coat closer and braced myself against the cold till Bill, the driver, arrived.

"Let me off near Highland High, Bill. I'm teaching about Lewis and Clark and Thomas Jefferson today and don't want to be late."

Bill and I had a morning routine.

"You have any trouble with those kids?" He started the conversation the same way for the third day in a row. I grinned and came up with a different answer every time.

"Nah, they're all right. A couple of the big guys in special education lean way back in their desks and I correct them. They bang the metal legs down as loud as they can to show off. A few minutes later we go through it again. I don't want anyone hurt on my watch, you know."

"So, you use the same material for regular kids and the slow ones?"

"The lessons move at different paces, and the regular classes go into more depth. They have different books, and I draw word pictures everyone can understand. We have a good time in my classes, and my supervising teachers usually leave me to do what I want."

Bill shook his head. "How do you get ready for each day, and how'd you get through college in the first place?"

"My fiancée helps, and I have volunteer readers who meet with me in the afternoons. The college told me to teach American history. I studied political science and world history, so I'm having to get up to snuff on our American heroes and laws."

"That's OK for now, but how'd you read your books the other years?"

"I figure I've had about 300 volunteers from several groups. Some came only a time or two, but others read for three or four years."

"Well, you must be easy to get along with. Makes me feel good to know there are that many unselfish young people. Here we are. You have a good day and make those big guys learn."

I clapped him on the shoulder and headed for the school, a brick building about a dozen years old with students from military bases and middle-class housing areas. Highland was Elaine's alma mater, so I was happy to be there. My graduating class from

NMSVH was composed of four students. Elaine had 699 in hers, a miniature city, but nothing I could not handle.

As usual after teaching, I rode back to UNM for my own classes and to study, then met Elaine when she got off work at a downtown bank. We took the bus to the base, where she read students' papers or texts for classes I was taking. That was the way it was supposed to work, but she needled me when she was bored by saying, "I hope we can do something fun tomorrow night." That was my clue that her patience was gone. It was time to go for a walk, play a game, get something to eat, anything but study, even if we had not yet finished. Maybe I could catch the rest with readers. Tomorrow would be our movie night.

About halfway through practicum, we decided I would make a formal request for her hand. She had worn my engagement ring for several months. Elaine left me with her father all afternoon while she and her mom visited her mother's millinery instructor and examined the latest styles of hats. I sat talking to Pop Carson, sweating it out alone. The day faded into evening. He put on no lights.

He told me, "She's very young, you know."

Smugly, I responded, "I plan to raise her to suit myself." I was confident I could.

There were silences with little small talk. Puff, puff on our pipes. The smell of Peach Brandy and Cherry Blend tobacco hung in the air. The colonel finally told me, "I know you don't have sight like most do, but you have traits that far surpass those of others she could marry. You can give her things they can't."

Elaine and her mother returned to a darkened living room and my elated heart. Elaine's parents were transferring out of state and would not leave her in Albuquerque unmarried, so our wedding would be the week after graduation. We had dated for almost two years.

Mom and Dad came the next month to meet Elaine's parents, and Dad commented that Pop Carson had very kind eyes. I was surprised to hear that because I could not see Pop's eyes, but I knew he was gentle and not haughty as some officers seemed to be.

I wondered if my dad had kind eyes. He might have, because he told me a father ought to give his son his first car and asked me if I would like to have his copper and white '57 Chevy Bel Air. My heart soared, and my fingers twitched in excitement.

They were probably twitching on my last teaching day, too. Even though I was well prepared, things did not go smoothly. My sister, Jo Ann, sat in on the class, but she was not the problem. Even the best students passed notes and whispered. I moved nearer the commotion, but behaviors escalated to scuffling and laughing in other parts of the room. Pencils flew. A book struck the floor with a loud noise. It was confusing. Why they misbehaved, I had no idea. The end-of-period bell rang, and they settled down. I let them go. Jo Ann said she always had hated history, but mine was the best lesson she ever heard. She liked the way I continued with the lecture despite interference. I apologized for the kids. I felt I had done all the right things.

I learned the explanation from two students when I came to observe my supervisor teach for a couple more days.

"Mr. Montague, we're sorry we were so bad on your last day, but the teacher said he wanted to see how you'd handle problems," the taller girl said, sounding anxious.

The other girl looked away and her shoulders drooped. "We feel guilty about it."

I had been set up.

During my final evaluation, my supervising teacher congratulated me for being six weeks farther ahead than he was in another regular education class. I had done what I thought was expected of me, and the group kept up.

However, student teaching left me frustrated that I should have done better, and I questioned whether teachers' expectations were high enough. When I was told to observe girls in gym classes working out on mats however they wanted, I wondered if they learned much. I talked with students about different exercises they were practicing. The regimen was much more rigorous at NMSVH.

What's more, I learned there was only one visually impaired instructor already in the school system, even though it was among the largest districts in the United States. By the time I finished practicum, the dean who said I never would teach in Albuquerque was the city's superintendent of schools.

As I prepared for final exams, the pace and excitement of parties, dances, and wedding planning increased. During Town Club's spring formal, we both received a huge surprise when we heard my name as recipient of the coveted "Town Club Favorite" award. It was a moment of disbelief followed by euphoria. The girls who had given so much to me gave even more.

Town Club dance

By Memorial Day, I was finished with practicum, and Elaine obtained her driver's license. We rode the Trailways Bus to pick up our new car. The San Jon community astonished us with a large bridal shower. We loaded gifts into the Chevy. Dad, Elaine, and I squeezed into the front seat. He did not want Elaine driving on the holiday weekend. We had all we needed to start our life together, plus $300 in savings. She had a job that paid $200 each month. Earning a Bachelor of Arts degree in secondary education was my entry to a bright future. Only one other person in my extended family of twenty had done that. Mom sent a special letter.

Dear Son,

It makes me sad, in a way, that this will probably be my last letter just to you. I'll no longer have a little boy, for he will be a man with responsibilities. However, I'm looking to the future and wish you and Elaine such a great and happy life together. Then I will not have lived in vain.

I was so proud and happy when you got your degree on Wednesday night. I guess we know what it took to get it, don't we? I hope to see you get another one someday! Or two more!

We'll be seeing you Friday. Until then, God bless you, and it's been so nice having you for a little boy. I know you'll be a fine man.

Love, Mother

She and Dad came for graduation. It was the happiest day of my life when Sylvia, a Town Club reader, handed me my university diploma.

Elaine and I introduce Mom and Dad
to Bob Carson on Sandia Base in Albuquerque

Tood and Hazel Montague

39 WEDDING

I walked confidently to our rehearsal dinner. I had not asked the bus driver, "Which way to the chapel?" Too late I realized I could not find it. I didn't understand why since Elaine and I had been there for church many times. I looked at my watch. Late. Very late. I should have asked Ryan or Steve or Lindy to bring me. Ryan was my best man. Steve and Lindy would light candles and usher. Jim, my longest San Jon friend, would have picked me up. Were the folks and Jo Ann already there? I could have asked my reader, Sandy, for a ride because she lived near the apartment and was our Maid of Honor.

Why didn't I plan? I worried about what Elaine's father must be thinking. What was she going to say? I felt more and more anxious.

A car pulled up. "Hey, Gary. Want a ride?"

"I sure do." Relieved, I sank into the seat of Ryan's car.

How embarrassing. Why did it have to be this way? I felt like a fool. I wanted to hide under a table when I arrived. Elaine had worked at the bank all morning before starting to prepare for the party. And she was on time.

Mom Carson served her Chicken Country Captain, a curry dish, and homemade yeast rolls. Traditionally, the groom's family hosts the rehearsal dinner, but my bride's parents were gracious to do it. Elaine and I were a bit oblivious to all the goings-on. We wanted to be man and wife and ignored the details.

Rehearsal Dinner - Elaine, Gary, Jo Ann

Sis was Matron of Honor, and Pop was our photographer. Over 300 people attended the wedding the next evening. Elaine's nine-year-old brother, Bob, cautioned them to untie the small organdy bags of rice with sprigs of lily of the valley before throwing them so as not to hurt us. The chaplain, father of a Town Club reader and Elaine's neighbor, became emotional while performing the ceremony. His voice shook, which was out of character. It was as though we were his own daughter and son.

I soon learned that I had not planned something important: our wedding night. We knew nothing of motels, so we stuck to Central Avenue, ending up west of downtown at a place called Globe Motor Court. Through the window, Elaine recognized the clerk as a boy she had had a run-in with in high school. She was embarrassed and refused to go in. I registered at about 9 p.m. It was so dark that night that we did not notice how ugly and worn down the place was until the next day.

Heading north out of town on U.S. 285, we navigated past much nicer motor inns. We had told no one where we were going. Elaine drove up the sharp incline of La Bajada Hill and through Santa Fe, then to Taos with its world-renowned New Mexico pueblo, the one built like a huge apartment building. We stayed at the Sagebrush Inn, which was top notch, rural, and south of town. Horses munched oats, making me think of my family's farm. Their smell wafting through the open window did not bother me. My city wife disagreed. We both laughed.

Going north again, we reached Red River by a treacherous unpaved washboard road with numerous switchbacks. I was pleased Elaine realized I was right about how beautiful the country was with its tall pines and steep mountains, where I had gone to 4-H camp as a boy.

Elaine got the hang of the Chevy and began life as our full-time driver. Between Red River and my folks' place, the clutch of our wonderful stick-shift Chevy stuck in second gear. It could only go forward, which was all right because we had no backup lights. Dad's mechanic thought he fixed the shifting before it was ours. None of it mattered. We had a wonderful time.

When we got home, her dad was incredulous. "You drove that road?"

40 GETTING BY

Elaine cooked a goodbye dinner for her family. They began their move across the country the next day. We were on our own, happy but finding it hard to pay for everything on $200 a month. We ate what she knew how to cook, which was mostly ground beef at forty-nine cents a pound. She began a better-paying job at a radio station until I received a call from a friend who told me to get her out of there because it was a bad situation. He was totally blind. How had he known? His job was to make reminder calls to businesses about upcoming meetings. When she answered the telephone, he was alarmed. I learned the new boss had a bad reputation with respect to young women. There were also criminal actions against the business. She quit that day.

For a month, we were both unemployed and kept it secret from our parents. One week, after paying our bills, we had thirty-two cents left, enough to buy a twenty-five cent Sunday paper. In late August, Elaine found a job, but her first paycheck did not come for a month. Our $300 savings account was almost empty. A five-dollar bill in a birthday card supplied what we needed after I cashed in a small insurance policy. Then the Chevy required a $300 repair. The dealer said my wife could not pick up the car because we had no credit and could not pay the bill. Plucky Elaine told him she was taking the car and applied for credit. We paid a little each month. We were never late with rent or other bills but often removed food from the grocery cart, humiliated just before checking out.

We also had harsh words. She did not believe I tried hard enough to find a job. I felt like I did everything possible. She could not conceive that no one would hire the "young-bright-educated-energetic-sincere-honest-hardworking" man with whom she had chosen to spend her life. She believed in me. Neither of us entertained the notion we had made a mistake. My ego hurt badly.

I could not find a job from mid-1960 through 1962. It was not an ideal way to begin a marriage. We isolated ourselves from friends.

Looking for work reminded me of when I first came to the city, only this search lasted a whole lot longer. Interviews often began with promise but fizzled.

"Tell me about your training. What skills do you have?" they would ask.

"I have a degree to teach high school social studies and government, and I'm eager to learn whatever you need me to do."

"Maybe you can use some of those skills here. What work have you done?"

"I grew up in the building trades and worked hard with

long hours. I know tools and had years of shop classes. I'm very responsible. You can depend on me."

"Who did you work for, and how much did they pay you?"

I told about being an interpreter in the fields, stocking at the grocery store, and working with Dad. I knew I worked methodically and solved problems as they arose. I understood a lot about criminology and sociology and could meet individual needs in educational settings before they were being widely addressed in public schools. My memory was excellent, and I needed to be told what to do only once.

None of it was what they wanted.

One man told me directly, "I admire what you have accomplished. You have conducted yourself very well in this interview and would be an asset to our company. I am sorry that there is no way I can hire someone with so little eyesight. I hope you have better luck somewhere else."

I knew next to nothing about seeking employment, writing resumes, or selling someone on the idea they needed me in their establishment. I did not know the longer I was unemployed, the worse I looked as a prospective employee. My confidence waned as the shadow cast by minds that believed visual impairment meant "not capable" obscured my future.

I asked myself how I could get their attention and persuade them that I could perform a job as well as anyone else and show them by doing, leading by example. Above all, could they understand how much I wanted to succeed in their sighted world? To have a career with dignity and acceptance?

Even though I grew up at my alma mater, I did not want to teach at NMSVH. I felt I needed experience and special training for that type of setting. But I sent a letter to Dr. Quimby anyway. He had no openings. In a short time, I learned he was ill. Then I heard he died.

After passing a difficult face-to-face federal examination, one which was not often given orally, offers were scant. Months after the test, I was offered a position as a social worker in New York City. I was not prepared for such a change and declined.

A finance company suggested I seek out miscreants to collect outstanding debts. And, oh yes, I would need transportation and a gun. That sounded impractical and far too risky for me.

A sales company showed me graphic films with which I was to scare or shame potential customers into purchasing home fire alarm systems. It disgusted me to think I should frighten people into feeling guilty because they might let their children die. It took a lot of explaining to my wife to show why I could not try that job. She had trouble believing what they were doing.

An agent asked if I could sell life insurance. All those tabulations were beyond my visual ability. What about peddling sets of encyclopedias door to door? With twenty-six large volumes and no car, the suggestion was preposterous.

We could not afford a private employment bureau, and that was the only kind we knew about. My parents had no idea how to navigate in our setting. Elaine's parents lived two thousand miles away. We were on our own and were no doubt clumsy. From the time I was eleven and all through college, Harold was my counselor from the state division of services to the blind and visually impaired. He produced only a few employment leads.

In those days, some citizens who were blind operated snack bars and vending stands in federal and state offices and public hospital buildings. The fellow in charge in New Mexico asked me to become a manager, but I refused because I knew I would find some way to use my education. I felt smart men and women without college should have opportunities to hold those jobs. He thought I was recalcitrant or arrogant and left me on my own. I depended on my friends who ran the stands to offer employment a day here, a day there, at one dollar an hour. Sometimes there were hazards. Once I backed into a large coffee urn. I can still feel the sting and heat on my skin. The stand was in a hospital, so a nurse came to my aid.

Meanwhile, my wife's income as a secretary was our mainstay. We persevered.

I thought about my skills. I touch-typed, read large print and a little braille, and used a tape recorder, Talking Book records and tapes, and a handheld magnifier. An ophthalmologist told me it was impossible for me to get around without a white cane or dog. Nobody at NMSB had used a cane or a dog. I did not realize how these guidance systems could help me. I feared they would arouse the shadow of social prejudice by broadcasting my disability.

During this period of unemployment, I met Dr. Hayden, an optometrist who instructed me in eye exercises and created optical devices to improve my vision. He was innovative and excited us with his sincere desire to help. He made a telescopic setup that looked odd but greatly improved my vision when I was sitting. It consisted of negative contact lenses and positive magnifying glasses. For reading, he clipped an extra set of bifocals onto the magnifying lenses. The extras had clear tops and additional magnification in the bottom halves.

When I walked, they made me nauseated. The glasses were heavy and would not stay in place despite an elastic band that went around the back of my head. Each movement changed my focal distance. More importantly, through the curvature of the thick lenses, I saw automobiles and other objects rush directly toward me. As successful as this setup had promised to be, it was not practical.

The doctor announced, "I've shot my wad. I have no more to offer. I'm sorry they didn't work."

Where would I find another vision specialist willing to tackle my low vision?

41 SANDIA YEARS

We stirred our drinks with TWA twizzle sticks, as a gracious stewardess served us snacks and a delicious full meal. Unfamiliar heat and humidity zapped us as we stepped out of the plane and waved hello to Mom and Pop that August in 1962. We wore lapel pins as souvenirs of the first-class Trans World Airlines flight to visit Elaine's parents. Little brother Bob, who was not so little anymore, led us to claim our bags at the Washington, D.C., airport.

The next day, Bob and Elaine climbed the Washington Monument in their tourist-like shorts and shirts. I had dressed to look as professional as I knew how because I met with the head of the United States Division of Services for the Blind. A secretary broke into the interview to inform me my children had arrived. I found Elaine and her brother waiting in the outer office.

A good chuckle was the only outcome of my effort to find a good job.

My diploma languished in my pocket in pristine condition for almost another six months before a promising interview and a final test in the parking lot of a large company. I met potential division and section supervisors and the company's doctor. They watched while I followed one's wave of an arm and general instructions to walk over and around parking barriers, through the gated chain link fence, beyond the theater, and into an office. Besides finding my way, I think they wanted to see if I could walk without tripping.

I quickly completed these tasks and became part of Sandia Corporation, or Sandia National Laboratories, and a member of the group of employees doing unclassified tasks while waiting for a security clearance. We were called the leper colony because we were restricted in where we could go and what we could see.

My shirt collar sported a photo badge clipped above a nerd pack of pens, including one with a wide black nib and another with a replaceable cartridge of dark ink. I had donned new shoes, with soles not showing wear from hitting the pavement, sharp-creased slacks, and a short sport coat, which was perfect given the mild fifty-five-degree New Mexico December day. Office mates ranged from scientists with a Ph.D. to administrative support, all eager to be cleared and begin the real work which our permanent badges would allow us to do.

My first task was to learn Sandia's mission and its proud history of nuclear weapons development, which began with the Manhattan Project in the 1940s, and to devise an inviting way to present its accomplishments to new hires like me. I was eager to prove how well I could do this. A secretary transcribed the words I recorded from a Dictaphone belt or a reel-to-reel tape recorder.

While I worked on the orientation, I remembered a legend I heard when I met Georgia Green during her return to our school. She had sight in only one eye from about age seven. The legend was that the last of her vision was sapped in July 1945 by an intense light she witnessed while being driven from Socorro, New Mexico, to Albuquerque during the atomic test at the nearby Trinity site—about fifty miles from the highway. It turned out she felt, rather than saw, the effects of the blast and there was no truth in the original story. The atomic test occurred a month before I went back to school, and it was reported as some other type of explosion. Then came the bombing of Japan and the end of WWII.

On graduation day from the leper colony, I was officially certified by the Badge Office as Gary-Ted-Montague-with-security-clearance, so I stood tall and found my new office building. Ziggy, the section supervisor with a wide smile and southern drawl, handed me a good cup of coffee.

"Here on out, it's up to you," he said.

42 BARE BONES

Sandia National Laboratories (SNL), a prime contractor to the U. S. Department of Energy, put me to work in the Training and Education Department. Tracking inventories of audio-visual gear of the Training Machine Shop, the Electronics Lab, and my department were challenging because numbers were inscribed on each piece of metal equipment for tracking. But the numbers might be located anywhere and had no color. Sometimes I used a mirror or asked another person to examine a piece with me. I accommodated so well that co-workers were surprised when they learned how limited my vision was. I set up and maintained records for the first time in my life and handwrote detailed five-by-eight-inch cards to track locations, acquisition and disposal dates, and condition of each piece. Elaine proofread my work at home when the slow, meticulous eye work exhausted me.

There were so many visual requirements that I persuaded management to buy a state-of-the art screen magnifier produced by Apollo Laser. It used a flat plate and closed-circuit TV to magnify what I wanted to read or write on. It was a new concept. I could move the flat part up, down, left, right. I rotated the lens by hand to change magnification. I looked straight ahead at the screen, ninety degrees from the paper, to read and write. The larger the print, the fewer characters I saw, slowing reading. It was a struggle, but I was happy to make progress, even though my best effort was not always appreciated.

I felt kicked in the gut when one supervisor told me, "I never would have taken you if I'd known how little you could see."

I also felt ashamed, angry, and puzzled—something like a descending roller coaster that gathers speed and heads for a shattering crash.

The crash came, but not as I feared, when I stepped off a curb which I thought was seven inches but was more like eighteen. It reminded me of a fall from a loading dock that had damaged my teenaged neck long ago. Off the curb and down I went in my new forty-dollar suit, tearing it and skinning my knee. I could not afford another suit, but my supervisor turned in a claim, and Sandia issued a check to replace it. I decided not to wear suits to work.

One afternoon, I offered to walk with a young woman I met in the office. I knew she rode my bus, but she said she was not leaving yet. When I boarded, she got on behind me. Did the lady think I would bite? It reminded me of when I was seven and struck up a conversation with a girl in my class at San Jon Elementary. Her father told me to leave his daughter alone. Some people act like a physical difference is contagious.

When I walked across the Tech Area to meet with a man about a new project I was to be part of, I lost my way back. It took me two hours to find my office. I endured quite a bit of good-natured ribbing from the guys. Seeing humor in the situation helped.

The inventories took a lot of time, but I thrived on assignments that allowed me to develop training courses, interview potential instructors, and advise in the operation of video programs and audio-visual equipment, procedures, and teaching techniques.

I worked for the Training and Education Division for fifteen years. That experience laid the framework for tasks assigned after I moved to the Safety Engineering organization as a Training Technician. I scheduled meetings and classes, created and operated a library of sixteen-millimeter safety films and videotapes, and advised supervisors about what to highlight in frequent mandatory and optional safety meetings, which were part of their annual job reviews. In my new office it was still a pen and paper world, but I took the Apollo Laser with me. I evaluated every item so that I could suggest appropriate media.

Pop Carson gave me a talking clock that I thought of as a novelty, but a 1980s talking wristwatch was one of my best purchases ever. I was proud to wear it every day.

Computers brought new ways to keep records. I could see the screen from about five inches. With design help from a good friend at work, I created, typed, and maintained a spreadsheet of all our educational resources and produced an annotated catalog. Finding ways to compile data into lists and records was always challenging. Thank goodness for pens with broad nibs and dark ink.

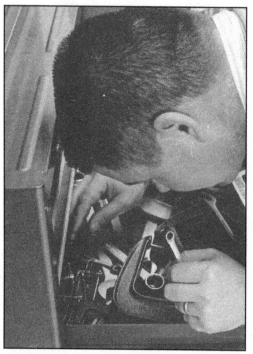

Gary at Sandia, peering into a toolbox

Twentieth anniversary, courtesy of SNL

Tenth anniversary, courtesy of Sandia National Laboratories

The telephone was essential to communication, but I used a cassette tape recorder on a special project requiring face-to-face conversations with security guards who worked the graveyard shift. We were to determine jobs for which these employees qualified once their health got to the point they needed to work with fewer physical demands and be inside, out of cold and heat. Guards came to my office, and we ended at midnight. My wife provided my transportation. The next work day began at the regular time. Being ready for the carpool was rough for a couple of weeks.

I neither expected nor received compensatory time or overtime pay. Supervisors listened to session tapes, and we discussed the interviews. Unfortunately, the recorder sat by the Apollo Laser and its buzz obscured the voices on some. As a result, I reported verbally.

Over the years, other assignments required me to be on site elsewhere. I flew to Tonopah, Nevada, to collect information about the Nevada Test Site that would be incorporated into a training video for use by the Nevada people and other organizations whose work interacted with theirs. Another employee and I traveled together because he had assignments near mine and helped me navigate transportation and the hotel. We each took care of business, then reconnected for the flight home.

This project excited me because I wrote the script for an important safety video. That led me to the Pressure Lab and the development of pressure safety training classes. My happiest and most productive times were when writing alone or developing courses with others, where I applied my teaching and curriculum skills. I was confident.

Our company offered continuing education to employees, but it was not easy to take advantage of the opportunities because of the lack of accommodations in the sprawling facility. The Apollo Laser was too large to take with me. For one mandatory class, I needed to provide my own transportation and readers all week. The city bus stopped near the training site. I hired three young women to read to me during the sessions and a co-worker took me back to the office, except for the day Elaine's student teacher, Charlotte, drove her compact car. I directed her over unpaved, rough terrain usually traveled by higher vehicles. The undercarriage hung up. She was not happy, and I was sorry to be such a poor navigator.

More years passed, and opportunities turned to frustrations, and advancement was elusive. Over and over, I asked for more challenging assignments. I was told to propose them, and my supervisor would decide if I could work on them. When I suggested new projects that had merit, they were given to sighted staff who reaped the fruits of my labor. I discovered that I came to Sandia with the education necessary for a staff member position. I knew I could do that job. Year after year, for three decades, I remained an administrative staff assistant. While people may sympathize, it remains a challenge for most to empathize and understand what it means to be artificially limited by low expectations and not have capabilities recognized.

When I was asked to attend a dinner at which the company honored an eminent European scientist who had become blind after becoming eminent, I thought I was invited just to show that my company had hired a "disabled" person. I went but wanted to be known for my abilities, not for a disability. Some years later, however, when I was asked to be the Handicapped Employee of the Year, I refused. I could not make myself accept the dubious honor of being singled out as a company token. It seemed to compromise my beliefs.

Despite such discouragements, Sandia changed our lives in many positive ways and was a good place to work with wonderful co-workers. After we were married for eight years, Elaine returned to UNM to pursue her lifetime dream of teaching, which would also include years of advanced training. For me, it was a personal best to be the sole breadwinner, able to give her what she wanted. People spoke to me with respect when they learned where I worked because the company was highly regarded.

Elaine student-taught in an elementary school classroom with ninety fourth, fifth, and sixth graders. It was the time of "open" classrooms, with three teachers to a pod, and all shared the children. Each had a student teacher, and Elaine needed a way to organize the students' work. We laid a Masonite bed board on the garage floor, the kind strong enough to go under a mattress and add support to a double bed but thin enough to accept staples. It had rounded corners, making it safer for the classroom. We measured carefully, then cut and attached horizontal strips of heavy, clear vinyl film. In the end, our board held ninety letter-size manila folders. She used the board that semester, then we hauled it over the next seven years to two more schools.

Twelve years after marrying me, she had her own classroom. At that school, I learned the librarian had no way to display colorful, small books. I love Christmas and borrowed an idea from the tree. Using light-weight pegboard with hooks and a metal spinning device, we built a book rack that turned easily and attracted children's interest. The smile I got from the librarian was a great reward.

We became good at measuring. Elaine included architecture in the curriculum, teaching young children to make scale drawings and bring to life creations in matboard or graham crackers. She built a scale model of our home, 1/8-inch equals one foot, which we used several times when remodeling or planning landscape projects.

We also became expert at visiting stores that were discarding or going out of business. Over the years, we hauled carpeting, display racks, matboard, and shelving to empty classrooms. We built bookcases and a windowed, four-legged, bright pink box for selling school supplies. Elaine was afraid of electric saws, so she checked measurements and I cut.

43 HER POINT OF VIEW

When a man or woman with full sight decides to marry a person with partial or no sight, some people wonder why. Over the years, Elaine persisted, "I was blessed with a loyal husband. You faced obstacles and discouraging roadblocks but usually didn't stay down long. You have always been fiercely independent, so much so that you suffer by not compromising your integrity. But these are the traits I love."

How could I not enjoy hearing she still has faith in me? It backfires a bit when she becomes upset if we run into someone whose social awareness about blindness resides in the Dark Ages. That kind will speak loudly to me or ask her, "What does he want?"

She refuses eye contact, ignores the question, or clearly says, "Ask him."

That is uncomfortable for me, but I love her intent. Some people act like I'm not intelligent, like they are surprised that I can reason for myself, or like I don't belong. They take a quick look and judge me. Despite progress in public understanding, there are a few negative rites of passage woven through the fabric of life. Maybe my story will help reduce occurrences of social prejudice or marginalization.

Some people stare as I try to read, act like I don't belong, or ignore me so that I feel isolated and out of the mainstream, much as I did in San Jon during high school summers. When I feel that way, powerless, I must guard against marginalizing myself.

I realize I was more marginalized before I went to the residential school than after developing skills and confidence there.

Other examples of marginalizing I experienced were assumptions I could not do a job or walk through a parking lot without falling, bullying by peers before I knew Spanish, my feelings about not being promoted or graduating with Jo Ann, and not being allowed a reader during college testing or getting plum assignments which could lead to advancement.

These behaviors show how much education still needs to be done among the general population.

My wife knows she needs to be specific. If she wants me to watch her purse while she steps away from the restaurant table, for example, I need for her to hand it to me because I may not see her set it beside me. She says, "Ramp up, ramp down," and "Curb up, curb down" with an estimate of inches when we walk. She scans the parking surface and warns me of hazards, like potholes, before I get out of the car. She gives clear directions or risks a surprise. One night, time suspended for her when she saw me enter the wrong gender-specific restroom at a dimly lit pizza parlor. I heard two women talking outside my stall, but it was too late to exit. As the banjo music played "Tiny Bubbles," Elaine waited anxiously for a woman to come out hollering. Luckily, I emerged alone.

A number of years after we married, we walked to the fairgrounds and Elaine demanded, "When are we getting a second car? Everyone I know has two cars."

Calmly, I asked her, "What would we do with it?"

She was dumbfounded when she realized there would be no need for two cars like the sighted couples we knew.

Elaine is very aware, however, of language and other forms of communication. The culture of the blind includes many everyday words and acts common to sighted brothers who use gestures and facial expressions. I do not see the raised eyebrows and animated looks of others but do raise my own eyebrows and use hand gestures.

Folk with no sight often part with the common phrase, "See you later." They may say, "I saw Johnny at the store the other day." Somehow, it seems incongruent to sighted folk when said by a person who is blind, but we talk the same way they do. When I listen to a recording of a book, I am reading. Dictating is writing.

Being able to speak Spanish sometimes helps when I am lost, take a wrong turn, or look down and miss seeing where my guide-wife went. It was more complicated than that when we visited Juarez, Mexico. She wanted to see how the people lived, not what was on display on the tourist track. We strayed into a neighborhood with a beauty shop, grocery, and residences with flowers and colorful paint. I was uneasy, but she did not worry because she trusted my Spanish. We got lost but found our way back to meet her parents, who were none-the-wiser about what we had done. Pop took us to dinner at an elegant Chinese restaurant where waiters wore white gloves. About midnight, he made a wrong turn while driving to the US-Mexico border. Pop let me out at a gas station to ask for directions from a non-English speaking attendant. I do not have a good sense of direction, cannot use a map, and was not as confident of my Spanish as they were.

People do not always call out but use gestures. I do not notice if a neighbor waves at me, but I lift my hand in greeting when I think one is close by. For weeks I waved at someone standing in a nearby yard but got no response day after day, only to find out it was a mop hanging on a fence, not a person at all.

It bothers Elaine that some people may think I am unfriendly. If I used a white cane or dog, they would grasp my situation quickly.

I have a lot of trouble with line of sight, the imaginary line from one's eye to a distant object, and that makes it hard to align the remote TV control. If I'm looking closely at the control, it's not looking at the box. Elaine must be patient while I find the channel.

I may be slower than she is when I set up and finish projects, but I work smarter, so she waits as I spend hours fashioning a part to repair something, thread pipe, or saw boards. I am happiest in my garage shop and take many things apart before discarding them, saving screws and investigating assemblage. I organize the tool chest drawer by drawer and hang items on the pegboard, separating long/short, heavy/light, and classifying by function. Memory and logic make tools easy to remove and put back. I find things when she needs them.

Leverage is not intuitive for Elaine. I understand how much pull I need to move and lift an object, how much resistance to raise a fifty-pound load, how strong a rope may be. When stacking items, not only do larger and heavier ones go on the bottom, but I must walk to the stowing area to make sure there is enough room; I cannot guess from a distance, as she does. I also must avoid hitting my head in the shop by keeping a hand in front or above me.

The gold standard is to ask how low vision impacts each situation. Then I might ask for help, experiment, or use a rod to test how far I am from the next object.

Elaine offers her arm to walk, but we also hold hands, thank each other for little things, pray together, and enjoy a quick smooch. Elaine says she respects me for my fortitude and what I have accomplished. It doesn't seem like much to me. We play little love games, like being first to wish "Happy Anniversary" each month on the right day. I buy her flowers. We quarrel, sometimes intensely. We agree to disagree on some issues and spend a lot of time together, but we enjoy a few hours apart. I worry, though, and call to ask if everything is all right, reminding her to stay safe. I don't know if this means I feel insecure, but I like it when she is here. I pray for her safe return when she's on an errand.

Elaine says my eyes are an attractive light blue-gray. She teases about the way my wiry gray brows furrow as I try to see, like the time I thought I saw a man bent over a bicycle, riding through the medical clinic. It was a man pushing a cart. That's the way it is in my reality.

"Sweetheart, sometimes when I'm depressed or disappointed," she tells me. "I wonder if my life would have been easier if I had chosen someone else, but I don't think I could have done that."

I'm tense but curious.

She says, "I'm convinced I didn't do the choosing. God did. You're not perfect. Neither am I. After all this time, I still say you are a winner. I thank God for placing you alongside me."

And for that, I am grateful.

44 WAS MOTHER RIGHT?

Just as many other people with long careers, I overcame adversity, obstacles, obstinate people, discouragement, and arbitrary rules, with some unfairness along the way, by minding my own business and keeping personal opinions to myself except when it became obvious I must respond. When I did not agree with supervision, however, I often chose to follow along because the boss is boss. At other times, I had to speak up because I knew a better way.

While I wanted no sympathy, supervision's attitude at times seemed to be, "Let him alone to fall on his face." I might feel ignored or had to ask for help. I concentrated on my tasks, sidestepped, and avoided situations that could get me into hot water. This applied to work and socializing, such as when staff members took long lunches during the popular "three-martini lunch" era of the 1980s, a practice I was not allowed to do.

At Sandia were unique characters, bright men and women full of information that I tried to absorb. I volunteered to teach employees whose English skills were poor, so they could earn a diploma equivalent to a high school education. They needed a GED for advancement. I also wrote the curriculum and taught in a community outreach program to help women on welfare gain skills needed to be employable.

Despite supportive associates and projects that I enjoyed, each day became more difficult as the decades went by. Nights were increasingly anxious. My sight diminished. I worried I was losing the little I had. As I approached my thirtieth anniversary at work, Mother was ill, and her letters contained frequent concerns.

Gary, what are you doing these days besides grinding your teeth over your job? Your mother grinds her teeth a lot, too.

We wish things would change for the better for you. You've had a "hard row to hoe" all your life, and never doubt that your mother knows you have. We're so glad Elaine can drive for you and help you do things.

Son, I'm concerned about your eyesight. Bosses can be beasts. I think they make it hard on their workers to make them retire early. I admire you very much for wanting to make it to thirty years, but if it ruins what sight you have, is it worth it? We do admire you and Elaine for what you've accomplished and are truly proud of both of you. I say prayers for you and hope earnestly that God hears them and will act accordingly. Life seems to get harder all the time, doesn't it? I hope and pray earnestly that things will get better for both of you.

"Oh, Mother, I'll be fine," I told her during a visit. "It's hard, but I can do it."

Over the next two years, however, I became frustrated with new shadows as I aged and found assignments less stimulating. The Americans with Disabilities Act had been law for four years, ever since 1990, but there were few accommodations. The Apollo Laser was housed down the hall from my office, making it less useful. I was told there was a space shortage.

I thought it would have been wonderful had there been a mentorship program to shepherd me toward growth over such a long time in the company. Despite no such program, Sandia had provided a good career with dignity. But it was time to change my life. I surrendered the security badge and enjoyed the end of a rigid schedule. I had done my best and was rewarded with a retirement based on thirty-two years of service. Sandia gave me a chiming wall clock as a remembrance.

I made a new life—traveled to beautiful places, tinkered and built things, and designed classroom items for Elaine. I looked forward to the future.

I also answered the longstanding question: Had Mom made the right decision that led us to board the train that had taken me to the New Mexico School for the Blind that chilly September night?

It had taken me a long time to appreciate her courage and the love she showed when she decided there was not an answer for me in San Jon, when she risked her marriage and trusted me to strangers.

The answer was, "Absolutely!"

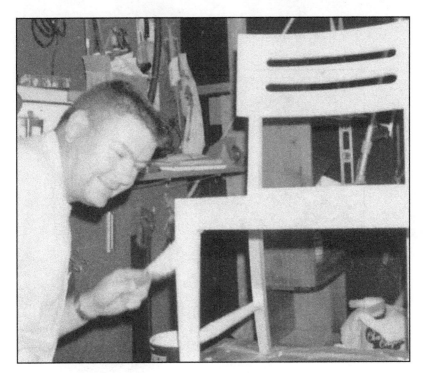

Gary's painting project

Mom and Gary on "that old sandhill"

Elaine with Ellen and Charles Carson

Well done, Mom and Dad Montague

WHAT YOU NEED TO KNOW

Flips, NMSB, courtesy of Nancy Tucker Collection

CONUNDRUM OF LOW VISION

When I was three, doctors told Mother that my visual acuity was 20/500. I had to be twenty feet from an object to see what most people saw at five hundred feet. I had quite a loss. I could not find the ball my twin sister tossed to me.

When I was finishing college, an ophthalmologist told me that 20/500 is what I see with my better eye and best glasses while the other eye sees half that well. To complicate my situation, my less good eye frequently overpowers my better eye. My vision flip-flops without notice, and then I do not see as much as 20/500. Sometimes I do not see the biggest letter on the eye chart. Since one eye sees or the other eye sees, I never have depth perception or much peripheral vision.

After I retired from Sandia National Labs, I had cataract surgeries. The doctor discovered the lens sacs had not formed properly, and she could not replace either lens. Later in life, a neurosurgeon tried to find out why I was having balance problems and said, "There's nothing there to work with, Sir." He said the occipital lobes also did not develop and showed me how dark they looked on a brain scan.

People sometimes ask me how I do everyday tasks. My own father told me he never understood what I saw until his eighties when he developed cataracts and suffered vision loss, which surgery restored.

After eight decades of living with low vision, I have strategies to navigate without getting hurt. Some are automatic, like feeling my way around with my hands or feet to determine distance or height of objects around me.

I listen for clues, too, like echoes. Because that does not always work, stress rises, and I am extra cautious. Sound helps me determine how far away moving cars or animals are and how quickly to get out of the way. With partial sight, it is tough to judge how wide I must open a car door, how low to bend for head clearance, or how high and far I must step. Therefore, I rely upon trial and error entering and exiting cars and trucks, same as I did with farm equipment when growing up. I might have gotten a few more pinches and hurts than a fully sighted kid would get, but I didn't notice.

Before I went to the New Mexico School for the Blind at age eight, I could not see the numbers in the books, and my poor arithmetic skills in school frustrated Dad. He unknowingly taught me a lot about geometry. We used ladders in construction, and he taught me how to use them safely. I remember his direction, Dad's law of physics.

"If yer gonna use a ladder, ya gotta learn how to set it up so's you don't fall off and the ladder doesn't fall down. Look here,

Boy. Set it so's the distance from a wall to the base of the ladder gives you a good, safe angle, and watch out fer how slick a surface is 'cuz they ain't all the same. And watch out for the molding."

Steps of ladders are shallow and house stairs more nearly match a person's foot from heel to toe. My ladder-climbing days are over, but I remember how I felt more secure on ladders with metal bottoms than on the older wooden ones we used at home because the metal tips moved and adjusted themselves on concrete. Through feel and experience, under Dad's watchful eye, I never fell off, although I thought I would when Elaine decided we should climb a long ladder to a cliff dwelling in Mesa Verde National Park, Colorado. That wooden ladder was not like my dad's, and I thought it was crazy that tourists were allowed on it.

On stairs, I reach for handrails and test depth and height. Angles of railings indicate steepness. I hear others on a stairway, and my own footfalls offer clues whether I face a lot of steps or a few. It's easier to judge on wooden ones.

People with vision changes must adjust ordinary activities. I hated giving up climbing onto the roof to service our swamp cooler several years ago. Until past middle age, I could see well enough to do that and could step off curbs in town without much difficulty if I tested them with a walking cane. I now travel with a companion.

When I used to mow the lawn, I tightened bolts, changed filters, added gas and changed oil, aligned the grass catcher, and made sure the clamps were caught, then cut in a pattern so I didn't miss spots.

Putting on shoes with Velcro is faster than tying laces.

While shaving, I use an electric razor first, then feel where the whiskers are, and finish carefully with a safety razor.

Modern T-shirt manufacturers use ink markings instead of tags, so I lay a shirt down to find the front, where the collar dips. On undershorts, the rib at center back is easy to feel, and there is a fly in front.

Being in public presents other problems. The contrast between outside light and the light inside a building results in total blindness that does not clear up for quite a while. When I enter a church, I cannot see pews or much of anything else as I find my way.

Dim lighting is also a problem, like in bathrooms and restaurants. Some public bathrooms have drains that make the floors uneven, and I may not know where the drains are. When my feet have my full attention, my head may ram into a column on a porch or the corner of an open cabinet door.

I walked alone with an IV pole at the hospital, but I could not see my feet or the casters. The pedestal's wide base reminded me of a 4-pronged walking cane that I did not like because it was a tripping hazard.

In the old days, Dad and I did not use terms such as geometry, friction, or physics when we solved problems, nor did we realize all the mental math I acquired at home. Helping Dad, who was called Tood Montague, was real-life learning, which gave me results I could see or feel or use. When I got to NMSB and I had trouble mastering braille with my clumsy fingers, it did not make sense to me not to use my eyes. Perhaps I also inherited a little of Dad's Tood-ness, a stubbornness born into the Montague men.

My parents taught me well without special guidance and taught me to figure out how to do whatever I had to do. NMSB taught me confidence and how to apply skills of independence. No one there said I could not learn, called me handicapped or disabled, or let me off easy. Sometimes I admit I feel exhausted with all the extra effort required, much as a wind-up toy whose key is missing, with no oomph, no go.

But then I remind myself to DRESS well and move on by remembering:

> **D**etermination is my base.
>
> **R**esilience is key.
>
> **E**ffort is required.
>
> **S**urvival is ensured.
>
> **S**uccess will come.

DEVELOPMENT OF TALKING BOOKS

Thomas Alva Edison in 1877 envisioned phonograph books that would speak to blind people without effort on their part.

The following information about the National Library Service is paraphrased and/or extracted from the article "Detailed History of NLS Talking Book Program," which was found online.

Embossed Books: Library services for blind patrons using books embossed with braille began in the late nineteenth century. In 1896, New York became the first state to create a department for the blind in a state library. A talking book record, which permitted thirty minutes of reading time on each record, was developed in 1933.

Records: In 1933, the American Foundation for the Blind produced two kinds of machines and a twelve-inch record with 150 grooves so that a book of 60,000 words could be contained on eight or nine double-sided records holding 15 minutes of reading per side. There was little format change in the original 33-1/3 rpm, twelve-inch, talking-book records circulated between 1933 and 1958, when two books were recorded at 16-2/3 rpm and could be played on existing machines.

In spring of 1962, the Library of Congress began ordering talking books for juveniles recorded on ten-inch records at 16-2/3 rpm, and all talking books ordered after January 1963 were recorded at 16-2/3 rpm. This smaller, slower-speed disc provided forty-five minutes of recorded time on each side, reducing the number of records required for each book. The savings effected by the change of speed were used to increase the number of copies of each talking book that could be produced and to add five popular magazines to the program.

In 1969, magazines began to be recorded at 8-1/3 rpm, and the recording of all disc talking books at 8-1/3 rpm began in January 1973. Use of these slow recording speeds made it possible to include almost twice as much material as on a disc of corresponding size recorded at 16-2/3 rpm. Since fewer records were required for each book, readers and librarians could handle, store, and ship the ten-inch, 8-1/3 rpm records much more easily and economically than the larger, bulkier ones.

Tapes: The first talking book cassette machines were widely issued in 1971. Each four-track tape cassette held six hours of playing time, about the equivalent of two hundred pages of print. Cassettes were recorded at 1-7/8 or 15/16 inches per second (ips). In 1980, a pitch-restoration feature was built in so that cassettes could be played at fast and slow speeds without a "Donald Duck" or a low-pitched drone effect.

Digital technology: Distributed in the twenty-first century.

LAWS AND GOVERNMENT

The Americans with Disabilities Act (ADA), 1990

The ADA of 1990 prohibits discrimination against people with disabilities in employment, transportation, public accommodation, communications, and governmental activities. Employers, such as Sandia National Laboratories, comply by offering accommodations and opportunities for advancement to veterans with PTSD and others with specific health conditions.

White Cane and Its Meaning

Although New York passed a law addressing the right of blind people to travel independently with a white cane in 1930, it was not until 1964 that there was a related national law. This Proclamation signed by President Lyndon B. Johnson authorized the President to declare October 15 of each year White Cane Safety Day. The white cane is intended to be a staff of independence for blind people. Marc Maurer, former president of the National Federation of the Blind, says with the white cane the "...blind are able to go, to move, to be, and to compete with all others in society...With the growing use of the white cane is an added element—the wish and the will to be free—the unquenchable spirit and the inextinguishable determination to be independent. With these our lives are changed, and the prospects for blind people become bright. That is what White Cane Safety Day is all about. That is what we do in the National Federation of the Blind."

Smokey Bear

U.S. Forest Service – Smokey Bear is used as a mascot to educate the public about the dangers of forest fires and wildfires. An advertising campaign began in 1944 and appealed to children.

Infant Mortality and Rate of Blindness

In the 1930s, the infant mortality rate in New Mexico was twice the national average, highest in the nation, and modern sewage treatment plants existed in only seven cities in the state. The NM death rate from syphilis per one hundred thousand deaths in 1945 was 10.6. Even in 1959, infant mortality in NM was slightly above the national average. Furthermore, the Social Security Bulletin of July 1953 reported New Mexico's rate of blind people per thousand as highest in the nation at 3.42, according to Ralph G. Hurlin, attributed largely to low health standards among parts of the population. Statistics are affected by the divergence among states in the definition of the term "blindness."

Corporal Punishment

New Mexico allowed corporal punishment, defined as discipline intended to cause physical pain, until 2011, when it was banned in public and charter schools. As of 2015, nineteen states continued to allow corporal punishment. Most common punishments were paddling, spanking, swatting with a ruler, shaking the shoulders, and slapping.

World Health Organization (WHO)

Two types of handicaps are defined by WHO:

1. Activity limitations, which occur when executing a task or action.
2. Participation restrictions, which are imposed upon an individual's involvement in activity.

CURRENT PROBLEMS
AND SOURCES OF ASSISTANCE

While progress has been made, Perkins School for the Blind reports results of a 2016 survey conducted by Research Now showing how much the misconceptions by people who can see create barriers to inclusion of those with loss of vision. The four barriers identified, called shadows by the authors, are discomfort, stigma, pity, and fear of sight loss. These barriers create artificial limitations for those with visual impairments. They are shadows which must be targeted to gain parity socially and in education and employment.

More people who are blind and visually impaired are seen more frequently in public today. Many more are independent with success in broader fields than when Gary graduated from UNM in 1960. They raise awareness in their areas of influence among those who encounter them. Due to limited experience with blind people and misconceptions among sighted people, however, false assumptions prevail. Awareness of the capabilities of the visually impaired by the general population is still lacking. Laws have been improved. However, public policy, limited accommodations, universal design, and inclusive standards do not always make the physical environment easier to navigate. Physical accommodations need to consider safety needs of those with poor or no vision.

Online support and chat communities of people with impaired vision encourage them to seek and share information. Individuals speak out to identify needs and improve the quality of life for themselves and others. The building of a community and international information-sharing are good. Many also write epubs, blogs, and print books, and gather in local support groups to talk about topics like macular degeneration, transportation, and services.

Today's technology offers audio books, online books, smartphones, and many assistive devices. Websites and videos explain and demonstrate application of concepts, but hands-on training in the use of devices is not easy to find unless one is in school. More senior services are needed as people live longer, resulting in a greater number of older persons with vision loss. Such elders have much to contribute to society which needs to be capitalized upon even after sight loss.

Assumptions about appropriate education of children have changed since the author's experience. In specialized schooling, creative educational programming implements strategies that teach to a child's strengths while compensating for weaknesses. Phenomenally, medical science offers hope for overcoming physical limitations by programming instruction to tap sight which is latent so that it may be used.

While there is much value in hand labor, gone is the heavy emphasis on manual skills, like making baskets and brushes.

Gone is the belief that using whatever sight remains could result in total blindness.

Gone is the belief that blind students should be separated by gender to avoid marrying one another, fearing they would produce children with visual impairment at a much higher rate than in the general population.

Today's model of education looks less at the economics and efficiency of instructing children in a centralized location away from their parents for long periods of time. The focus is more on family dynamics and keeping children with their sighted peers in their home communities. As students are educated in their local schools with assistance for them and their teachers, inclusion replaces residential school experiences like the author had. Transportation has improved so that brief stays at a residential school to develop special skills are available. Students who need more time and intense instruction in a residential school are often able to spend weekends at home with family.

Both education and employment of those with visual impairment, however, remain problems. Obtaining texts and accessing resources in a timely manner and useful format are often difficult. Support for a student with a print disability varies widely because of many factors, one of which is whether there is help from a disability resources office. Others include how much the student is involved, responsiveness of publishers, time required to convert materials, wide range of individual needs, changes in courses and types of course materials, and delays.

Regrettably, today's challenges are not very different from the trouble Gary Ted Montague had getting texts and supplemental materials on time and in an accessible format. Although recent studies by commissions and BISG (Book Industry Study Group) have been reported to the U. S. Congress, few accessible materials are readily available for purchase or easy to acquire. Some textbook committees recommend adopting only epubs which do not need conversion and can be read with a screen reader.

Inclusion, services provided, and fulfillment of goals set in Individualized Education Programs (IEPs) for individual students must be monitored carefully by parents and compliance officers to ensure a free, appropriate, public education. Those providing service must be trained and competent. The National Federation of the Blind reported over seven million adults with visual impairment in 2015, with only one million employed full time. Fewer than 15 percent had earned at least one college degree, and many had not finished high school.

Abundant information and products are available from sites such as the American Foundation for the Blind (AFB), National Federation of the Blind (NFB), American Printing House for the Blind (APH) Connect Center, state commissions for the blind, and social media support groups within the community. Blind New World of Perkins School for the Blind seeks to erase stigmas by showing all of us ways to interact successfully as and with those with vision loss. Books in alternative formats are offered by state libraries through the National Library Service Talking Books Program and private companies, such as Audible, Learning Ally, LightHouse for the Blind, The Blind History Lady, and Horizons for the Blind. The international advocacy group, World Blind Union, works for advancements in the mobility, education and independence of blind and partially sighted persons. APH has established The Hall of Fame for Leaders and Legends of the Blindness Field.

The strength of long-standing advocacy organizations like the American Council of the Blind, the National Federation of the Blind, and the American Foundation for the Blind continue to grow and become more capable, and such associations warrant support.

ABOUT THE AUTHORS

www.elainemontague.com
https://binged.it/2jzo1yc
authormontague505@gmail.com

Gary and Elaine Montague, a team for sixty years, share this personal story to show why there is no giving up! They want people to know there are degrees of blindness and understand more about the challenges of low vision, sometimes called partial sight.

Gary Ted Montague has coped with low vision since birth and desires to be recognized as a man able to participate fully in life, to be measured by who he is instead of by low societal expectations. He knows the heartache of separation from family, the frustration of difficult challenges, the importance of personal faith, the success of achievement, the warmth of kindness, the relief of hard work, and the joy of academic and career worlds.

As a college graduate with a Bachelor of Arts Degree in Secondary Education, he advised and taught sighted adults in a major scientific lab for 32 years. He worked in the areas of Education and Training and Safety Engineering. When

Albuquerque Public Schools set up special education programs for vision in the 1970s, Montague convinced them to use the term visually impaired and not use the word handicapped. This is the first telling of his story. When he and his wife presented their work to an alumni group from the New Mexico School for the Visually Handicapped (formerly, New Mexico School for the Blind and now called New Mexico School for the Blind and Visually Impaired) and other schools, listeners expressed gratitude that someone is finally telling their story.

Historic Albuquerque Incorporated (HAI) produced a video of Gary's oral history, part of which was presented at the 2018 annual conference of the Historical Society of New Mexico, of which he is a member, and put it online. It is to be placed in repositories at the University of New Mexico's Center for Southwest Research, the New Mexico State Records Center and Archives, the Albuquerque Public Library Special Collections, and the Albuquerque Museum of Art and History.

Elaine Montague, his fully sighted wife, taught children and trained adults for 31 years in Albuquerque Public Schools. Her students included intellectually gifted children and those with learning challenges due to learning disabilities, emotional/ behavioral problems, and communication disorders.

Elaine's creative work includes public speaking, writing short articles, curriculum development, and application of unusual strategies to teach children. She is published in *SouthWest SAGE, Resources in Education (ERIC)* and *Educational Technology* and

presented original work at a national conference of Council for
Exceptional Children. She was honored as Computer Educator of
the Year, New Mexico Council of Computer Users in Education,
and nominated for Disney's American Teacher Award for
creativity in teaching.

With degrees in regular education, special education, and
educational administration, she taught children in grades 1-6,
trained regular and special education teachers K-12 in classroom
use of computers and modification of materials to meet individual
learning needs, initiated innovative programs for adults and
children, and contributed to grant applications and curriculum
guides. She authored *Birthdays Are Ageless,* about forty years
of celebrations by four friends. For six years, she facilitated a
memoir writing critique group.

A team for sixty years, they have published separately and
together and won local, state, and national awards for their
writing.

Gary at NMSBVI Centennial, 2003

QUESTIONS FOR DISCUSSION

1. Think about a job you have had in or out of your home. What accommodations would be needed so your job could be done by a person who is blind?

2. How is your knowledge different now from what it was before you read Gary's story?

3. How are you better equipped to advocate for a young child or older parent with a vision loss? Think in terms of education, employment, or physical accommodations in public places.

4. The model of schooling has changed since Gary enrolled at a residential school for the blind in 1944. If you had a child with low vision, how would you want his special needs met?

5. Driverless cars and corneas made by 3-D printers look promising. What kinds of advancements or accommodations do you think could improve a blind person's quality of life and ability to perform well in the workplace? Which do you see happening in your lifetime?

6. Who would benefit from reading "*Victory from the Shadows*" in the next three months? How can you share another copy or your own?

INDEX

Dear Reader,

We hope you like Victory from the Shadows and find it useful. You can do something important, and it only takes a moment or two. Leave a review on Amazon.com. It does not matter if you purchased your book online or somewhere else. Your opinion counts and will help many others.

Sincerely,

Gary and Elaine Montague